Capturing and Keeping the Pastor's Heart:

How to release your blessings through service in ministry

Apostle Jamie T. Pleasant; Ph.D.

Capturing and Keeping the Pastor's Heart:

How to release your blessings through service in ministry

Apostle Jamie T. Pleasant; Ph.D.

Capturing and Keeping the Pastor's Heart:

How to release your blessings through service in ministry

ISBN-978-0984374816

Table of Contents

Releasing Your Blessings

You gave your life to Jesus Christ and joined a church. Now you're ready to serve and reap the benefits of ministry work — blessings in your life! In order to receive everything God intended for you, capturing the heart of the Pastor or ministry leader of your church is essential to your success.

Best-selling author Apostle Jamie T. Pleasant; Ph.D. brings you *Capturing and Keeping the Pastor's Heart: How to release your blessings through service in ministry.* This is an eight-week study on how to serve faithfully and under the anointing of the Holy Spirit in your church. You'll learn how to capture your church leader's heart and give it your all in ministry as you work with other church members to build up the body of Christ.

This book is designed for your personal growth as well as small group Bible study. Each week, you'll get a deeper revelation on how your blessings are tied to your ability to serve your church leader and others with your whole heart. Chapter exercises and key points will help you make the most of your study time as you discover the keys to releasing blessings in your life.

Dedication

To my daddy Anthony T. Pleasant who was a perfect example to me of a real man. To my wife Kimberly, my two sons; Christian and Zion, and daughter, Nicara

To the New Zion Christian Church family, especially, Celeste Dickson, LaCretia Jones, Latoya Dockery, Deacon Lyndon Earley, Minister Lawrence Gibbs III, Pastor Timothy Brown, Sequester McKinney, Deacon John F. Kennedy, Tiffaney McCutcheon and Pastor Raymond Dockery.

Humbly Yours, Apostle Jamie T. Pleasant

Getting the Most from
Capturing and Keeping the Pastor's Heart

Congratulations on purchasing this book! Get ready to take your service in ministry to the next level. You can use this book for personal or group study. All of the scriptures are from the New International Version, or NIV Bible translation (unless otherwise noted). You'll find it helpful to have your Bible handy as you study.

This book includes eight chapters — perfect for a week-by-week study or reading at your leisure. In addition, you'll find:

- **<u>Key points -</u>** Each time you see a box with words in italics inside of it, this means that an important point has been presented that you should pay careful attention to.
- **<u>Response sections -</u>** Each time you see a blank underlined section on a page, you should jot down your thoughts and reflections as it pertains to the teachings.

Chapter 1

Opening Your Heart to Be Blessed By God

I pray also that the eyes of your heart may be enlightened in order that <u>you may know the hope to which he has called you, the riches of his glorious inheritance</u> in the saints

Ephesians 1:18

The first key to unlocking your blessings is to capture your Pastor's heart. Capturing your Pastor's heart means that you are properly aligned in the spirit with the leader that you serve together with in your local church. This is the first key step in gaining a better understanding of your role and your Pastor's role within your church. The important truth to remember here is that prayer initiated by your Pastor begins the process of you being able to receive your Pastor's heart. Your Apostle or Pastor has to pray for their heart to be received by you and only the Holy Spirit can make that happen. Did you get that? Capturing your Apostle's or Pastor's heart is not something you initiate; it begins with them praying for you to receive their heart. Our job is to open our hearts to capture the blessings they want to share with us. And this transfer of blessings that they want to share can only happen through prayer.

1

> *Capturing your Apostle's or Pastor's heart is not something you initiate; it begins with them praying for you to receive their heart.*

What a beautiful scripture in Ephesians 1:18 where it shows us how Paul, an Overseer, Pastor and Apostle of Christ Jesus is praying for his followers. Paul is pleading that the eyes of their heart will be opened to see a hidden spiritual reality that was not shared with many at that time. He prays that the eyes of their hearts will become enlightened in order for them to see a great hope that awaits them. He prays that their eyes can be opened to see the hope of their calling. And, with that calling comes the hope of great blessings from God. He knows that their blessings are tied up in their ability to respond to their ministry calling in the local church. He knows that in order for them to walk in a new found completeness and divine blessing, they must begin to operate in the purpose of their calling by serving in ministry with their spiritual gifts. First, let's look at a great revelation here. Paul wants the eyes of their hearts to be enlightened. Did you see the blessing in what he said? Our heart does more than beat a certain number of times per minute. Our heart does more than pump blood to other parts of our body. It even goes beyond just serving the purpose of keeping us alive.

Our heart actually has eyes. That's right! Our heart was designed by God to see certain things beyond the level of natural eyesight.

God designed our hearts to be able to see beyond circumstances and present situations we may be facing. Our hearts have the ability to see into the beautiful realm of hope. The word hope, which in the Greek is pronounced *el-pece*, means to anticipate usually with pleasure; expectation and confidence. Paul is praying for the members of the church of Ephesus who are placed under his care. God has given Paul a blessing. Paul prays this blessing on the people to allow their hearts to become enlightened to have the ability to see hope.

Please grasp the truth here that Apostle and Pastor Paul is praying a blessing on his people! He is praying that they may become able to walk into a new reality of seeing, knowing and embracing hope. Note that the people under his care never knew this existed. They only learn about this revelation as Paul prays it for them to know. This is a truth we must never forget: The Apostles and Pastors God places in our lives are here to open spiritual realities. These realities that we never knew existed are revealed through the leading and teaching of the Holy Spirit.

> *The Apostles and Pastors God places in our lives are here to*
>
> *open spiritual realities.*

Please also note that Paul is simply sharing with his people what God has already shared with him. He is taking what is his and making it available for those serving with him in the local body of believers. Paul is not praying this prayer for anyone who might hear it. He isn't praying this prayer for those who want to go to a higher level in life. No! He is praying this prayer for those who serve with him at the local church who recognizes him as the leader and overseer. He is talking to the people who belong to the local church of Ephesus. He is blessing them with a revelation that will take them to a new level in life as they serve with him and under him in ministry. And just like Paul, the Apostle or Pastor of a church must pray for us to see spiritual realities and bless us with what God gives the church leader. The Apostle or Pastor must pray for us to capture their heart.

Through his prayer, Paul is giving them his heart. He is giving them his vision. He is giving them his gifts. He is giving them everything that God has given him. We should all realize that as we serve with God's called Apostle or Pastor, God will move on that Apostle or Pastor to share the blessings with us that have been given to him/her. It is important that church members desire to have the same heart of their Apostle or Pastor.

Also, notice that one of the main responsibilities of a Pastor is to get you to a place where you can hope for better things: a better life, a better job, a better marriage, etc. Paul wants the church at Ephesus to learn how to see beyond personal problems and limiting circumstances and walk in the blessing of seeing hope. He doesn't want them to get stuck in the reality of a disorganized life, a personal heartbreak and/or challenging circumstances. Paul wants those who have been placed under his care to be able to anticipate a positive, pleasurable, expected end knowing that God has a better plan for their lives. He doesn't want them to focus on the reality of what they are experiencing at the moment.

This hope is a revelation and a blessing for the church of Ephesus. How can a church walk in the blessings of God when there is no flowing of revelation from the Holy Spirit to the Apostle or Pastor that ultimately reaches the people? A revelation, or the ability to have hope, is a gift for the body of believers. This revelation can only come through the teaching of the Holy Spirit through an Apostle or a Pastor.

The Flow of a Revelation and Blessing from God

God gives the revelation and blessing to the Holy Spirit
↓
The Holy Spirit transfers the revelation and blessing to the Apostle or Pastor
↓
The Apostle or Pastor transfers the revelation and blessing to the people serving with him/her

---

Why is it important for Paul to pray for his people? They must have his heart to receive a blessing from God. If they are under Paul's care and direction, their blessings are locked up with their ability to capture Paul's heart. When you put all of this together, it shines light on the truth that there is a gifting, blessing and power that flows through the anointing of God to the Apostle or Pastor to the people who are called to serve with and under him/her. It is true that the anointing flows from the head down.

Now, let's see how the anointing flows from the Apostle or Pastor to the people. **Psalms 133:1-3** says,

How good and pleasant it is when brothers live together in unity! It is like precious oil poured on the head, running down on the beard, running down on Aaron's beard, down upon the collar of his robes. It is as if the dew of Hermon

were falling on Mount Zion. For there the Lord bestows his blessing, even life forevermore.

We can see clearly here that there is a flowing of blessings to the people of God from the High Priest, Aaron. This flowing starts from God, is transferred through the Holy Spirit and ultimately all the people of God serving with and under Aaron are blessed. A blessing is given through the unity of the people. It is the unity of the people that causes the flow to start.

The gifting, blessing and power that flows through the anointing of God to the Apostle or Pastor to the people can only come through unity.

Unity means to become a unit, to act as one, to come together and oneness. Please note that unity doesn't mean sameness but oneness. Now we must grasp the truth that oneness means uniqueness. Psalms lets us know that it is each believer's uniqueness that causes the unity to exist in the body of believers. This means we must get along with each other and then accept each other's uniqueness.

Unity doesn't mean sameness but oneness.

Let's take a look at an example of how unity and uniqueness are displayed through the teamwork of sportsmanship. One of the most successful basketball teams of all time was the Chicago Bulls of the 1990s. Particularly, the championship team of the 1990-1991 Bulls is a good example of the power of uniqueness. The main players of the championship team were Michael Jordan, B.J. Armstrong, Bill Cartwright, Horace Grant, Scottie Pippen and John Paxson. Others on the championship roster included, Cliff Levingston, Craig Hodges, Stacey King, Will Perdue, Scott Williams and Dennis Hopson. The head coach was Phil Jackson.

None of these guys were built the same or were the same height. They didn't even shoot the basketball the same. For example, Bill Cartwright was the worst shooter on the team. His shot was the most awful thing to look at. At the same time, Michael Jordan's jump shots were a work of art and perfection. By the way, Bill Cartwright was 7'1"; Michael Jordan was only 6'6". Now here is where the power of unity comes in. While Cartwright couldn't shoot a jump shot to save his life, he could rebound like no other in the NBA. Not only was he tall, but he had very long arms for his height. His arms and torso were longer than the rest of his body. That is why he had such a hard time shooting the ball. His arms were so much out of proportion to his body that he had a hard time getting in rhythm. When it came to rebounding a ball however, it was a work of art to watch. He would box out his opponent and really not have to jump at all to get the ball. He would just position himself between his opponent and the basketball goal, then stretch out his hand and the ball was his. Michael Jordan couldn't do that. He had to really jump (and he could) to get the rebound. Jordan was a much better shooter than he was a rebounder.

Notice how Cartwright was so awkward at shooting but graceful and so effective at rebounding. We need to be reminded that when it comes to serving in the local church, we may be awkward at one thing but yet gifted, graceful and very effective at other things. Think of ministry as a team effort. We all have a part to play, and none of us are gifted the same way. We are all unique. When we get along and serve as one, each adding our unique gifts, we can receive God's anointing from the Apostle or Pastor. Know that we may be awkward at one thing but excel at another thing in ministry. We must learn to pray and ask the Holy Spirit what is our role in a ministry or assignment given by the Apostle or Pastor. Once the Holy Spirit tells us our role, we must accept that role and do the best job we can to fulfill the purpose that God intended. We must keep in mind the overall result is that we must be very effective as we play our part offering our uniqueness to the assigned task at hand to achieve the overall goal of the ministry.

> *When we get along and serve as one, each adding our unique gifts, we can receive God's anointing from the Apostle or Pastor.*

Now remember, it is our Apostle or Pastor, who asks us to complete tasks. They are the ones who will help us find our place in ministry. At times, we may feel misplaced or misdirected by our Apostle or Pastor. We may feel like we should serve in other parts of the ministry. But if the Holy Spirit is leading us, we should welcome the direction of our spiritual leader. We should not be discouraged when we can't perform certain duties that we have been asked to do in ministry by our Apostle or Pastor. Again, we shouldn't feel we have been misplaced or misdirected by our Apostle or Pastor when we feel awkward or out of place in a certain ministry. We must trust that the Holy Spirit has placed us somewhere we feel awkward but we do bring a gifting and uniqueness that blesses the work of our local church.

Write down a time you can remember in your life where you were given an assignment or something to do, and you felt out of place or awkward.

_____

_____

_____

Now, write down how an awkward assignment that made you feel uncomfortable turn into a great blessing not only for you but also for the organization, group or project.

_____

_____

_____

God gives us assignments that sometimes will make us feel inadequate and uncomfortable. We must rest assure that He has given us the ability to complete all parts of the task through the work of the Holy Spirit. Just because some of the things we do may seem awkward and uncomfortable doesn't mean that we are not still needed to complete the overall task that God has called all of us to accomplish together. Guess who looked at the ability of all the players on the Bulls team and assigned their positions? It was the coach. It is his job to look at the strengths and weaknesses of each player and assign a position to each one of them. It is the coach's job to make those assignments and then turn around and develop the players to their fullest potential so they can be successful.

11

The Holy Spirit speaks to Apostles and Pastors. They will give assignments to people in ministry based on their individual strengths and weaknesses. The roles we are given in ministry may not be the ones we want, but they are the ones God gives. We must remember that those whom God calls, He also gifts. It is very easy to get mad when an Apostle or Pastor gives us an assignment that we don't like. However, we must remember to be careful not to lose the heart of the Apostle or Pastor. If we lose the Apostle's or Pastor's heart, we miss the transfer of God's anointing from the Apostle or Pastor to us. We are really being endowed and gifted to perform uniquely toward a given assignment for God. In other words, we need to be careful not to lose the Apostle's or Pastor's heart by not accepting the assignment that is given to us. Another way to look at it is to make sure we work wholeheartedly to perform and complete the assignment. Then we can grow in the blessings of God.

> *The Holy Spirit speaks to Apostles and Pastors to assign people in ministry based on their individual strengths and weaknesses.*

Again, Paul says in **Ephesians 1:18**:

I pray also that the eyes of your heart may be enlightened in order that <u>you may know the hope to which he has called you, the riches of his glorious inheritance</u> in the saints.

There is a calling that God has assigned to us that will release and unlock the riches of a glorious inheritance for the saints. Those riches are more than salvation. Those riches include peace, joy, love, health, wealth and other great things of God. We will be able to experience all of these great things as we respond positively to the call of God that is given and assigned by our local Apostles and Pastors. We must have their heart in order to receive the glorious riches to which we have been called.

Let's look again at the Chicago Bulls example. A major point must be made here about Jordan's ability to shoot. In the late 1980s and 1990s, Jordan shattered almost every point scoring record that stood in the NBA. In fact, the most points Jordan scored in a game was 69 in a 117-113 overtime win at Cleveland on March 28, 1990. It was unbelievable to watch one person score so many points in one game. Even with that amazing scoring by Jordan, most people never noticed how many times Cartwright pulled down offensive rebounds and gave Jordan additional chances to score. Although Jordan could out shoot Cartwright, he couldn't out rebound him. Cartwright could out rebound Jordan, but he couldn't out shoot him. Yet, without Cartwright, Jordan's points alone couldn't win a game. He got second and third chances to shoot and score because Cartwright would rebound the ball and give it back to him. After the games, most reporters would run up to Jordan and interview him and never ask Cartwright one question. This should have made Cartwright mad or even jealous. But it didn't. Cartwright knew that he had a role to play on the team and that role was to rebound and give Jordan extra chances to score. This is a lesson for all of us.

Our hearts must be open to accept the assignments from God and our Apostle or Pastor. When we do our part wholeheartedly, the ministry becomes successful. We should work to be good in whatever roles we are assigned. We may not all be like Michael Jordan. We may not even be like Bill Cartwright. As long as we are on the team and accept our assignments, the church benefits. We must make sure we guard our hearts from feeling left out and looked over if we don't like where we are assigned in ministry.

> *Our hearts must be open to accept the assignments from God and our Apostle or Pastor.*

We must learn to trust the Apostle or Pastor that God has placed over our lives. The job is not an easy one as he/she has been called to empower, develop and equip us. **Ephesians 4:11-13** says,

It was he who gave some to be <u>apostles,</u> some to be prophets, some to be evangelists, and some to be <u>pastors</u> and teachers, <u>to prepare God's people for works of service,</u> so that the body of Christ may be built up until we all reach unity in the faith and in the knowledge of the Son of God and become mature, attaining to the whole measure of the fullness of Christ.

As we accept the leadership of an Apostle or Pastor in our lives, God will then turn his/her heart to us. Our Apostle or Pastor will pray just like Paul that our hearts will become enlightened to receive the hope of future blessings that God has in store for us. We will then become a people doing works of service. We will be built up into a great unit where we too, just like the Chicago Bulls, will become champions — that is, champions for Christ!

Chapter 1 Review and Exercise

1. Capturing the Apostle's or Pastor's heart is not something we initiate; it begins with the Apostle's or Pastor's prayer.

2. The Apostles and Pastors God places in our lives are here to open spiritual realities.

3. The gifting, blessing and power that flows through the anointing of God to the Apostle or Pastor to the people can only come through unity.

4. Unity doesn't mean sameness but oneness.

5. When we get along and serve as one, each adding our unique gifts, we can receive God's anointing from the Apostle or Pastor.

6. The Holy Spirit speaks to Apostles and Pastors to assign people in ministry based on their individual strengths and weaknesses.

7. Our hearts must be open to accept the assignments from God and our Apostle or Pastor.

Spiritual Exercise

1. Write down the key things you have learned from this chapter.

   _____

   _____

   _____

   _____

   _____

2. Write a prayer to the Lord to help you develop a heart for your Apostle or Pastor.

   _____

   _____

   _____

   _____

   _____

Chapter 2

Works of Service, Blessed by God

It was he who gave some to be <u>apostles</u>, some to be prophets, some to be evangelists, and some to be <u>pastors</u> and teachers, <u>to prepare God's people for works of service</u>, so that the body of Christ may be built up until we all reach unity in the faith and in the knowledge of the Son of God and become mature, attaining to the whole measure of the fullness of Christ.

Ephesians 4:11-13

The Holy Spirit places Apostles, Prophets, Evangelists, Pastors and Teachers in churches for the primary purpose of **preparing God's people for works of service**. The word prepare comes from the Greek word, *katartizo*. *Katartizo* means complete furnishing, or the perfecting of a person. *Katartizo* also means to become one; together and unity. Let's take a deeper look at the word *katartizo*. Just as the Apostle's or Pastor's role in the church is to prepare us to serve, we also have a role to become prepared to serve. That's right! We have to be ready to be trained and equipped. We cannot be prepared to submit and serve until we understand how God moves through unity and oneness within the church.

19

The second key to releasing your blessings through ministry service is to understand that the church is the body of Christ. We can see this in **1 Corinthians 12:27-28:**

Now <u>you are the body of Christ</u>, and each one of you is a part of it. And <u>in the church</u> God has appointed first of all apostles, second prophets, third teachers, then workers of miracles, also those having gifts of healing, those able to help others, those with gifts of administration, and those speaking in different kinds of tongues.

We can get a clearer revelation of this truth by looking at **Ephesians 5:23:**

...as Christ is the <u>head of the church, his body,</u> of which he is the Savior.

Before we go any further let's make sure we understand what happens when we give our lives to Christ and join a church. When we accept Jesus Christ into our lives, become a believer of Christ and join a church, we become a part of His body.

> **The church is the body of Christ. When we accept Jesus Christ into our lives, become a believer of Christ and join a church, we become a part of His body.**

Ephesians 5:23 shows us that Christ Jesus is the head of the church. The same verse adds the truth that the church is His body. Now watch this! Not only is Christ the head of the church, which is His very own body, He is also assigned the responsibility to keep the church saved. When we give our lives to Him and become a part of a local congregation, our bodies become infused with His body and we become one with Him and the congregation.

Oneness or unity allows us to function in the fullness of His glory. In other words, we can't operate in the power of Christ without being a part of the body of Christ. However, being a part of the body of Christ is more than church membership and being saved. We have to be an active part of His body. We must do something for Him and with Him. Peter couldn't have healed people if he wasn't actively a part of Christ's body. Paul couldn't have raised people from the dead if he wasn't an active part of Christ's body. Stephen couldn't have worked miracles among the people if he wasn't an active part of Christ's body. We must grasp the truth that in order for us to flow in the power of God and receive the blessings of God, we must be attached and actively engaged in the body of Christ. Peter, Paul and Stephen had to be actively involved within the body of Christ in order to operate in the power of Christ. How did they get to this point to be able to operate in such power? They were instructed by the Holy Spirit and even Christ Himself. Someone had to train, teach and equip them to operate in the power of God.

Let's look again at **1 Corinthians 12:27-28:**

Now <u>you are the body of Christ,</u> and each one of you is a part of it. And <u>in the church</u> God has appointed first of all apostles, second prophets, third teachers, then workers of miracles, also those having gifts of healing, those able to help others, those with gifts of administration, and those speaking in different kinds of tongues.

Here we see that we are the body of Christ. In fact, the scripture clearly shows that we are a part of Christ's body. As members of the church, we must be actively involved in playing our part through ministry service. However, look at the next verse: In the church God has appointed first Apostles, then Prophets, then Teachers, etc. The scripture shows that the Apostles, Prophets, Teachers, etc. are ranked by their level of involvement in the body of Christ. In order for a body to operate, all parts must function correctly or the body is not able to operate at 100% capacity. Apostles and Pastors have a part to play in the body of Christ and so do we. However, we can't play our part if, as a member of the body, we aren't functioning correctly.

> *In order for a body to operate, all parts must function correctly or the body is not able to operate at 100% capacity.*

For example, have you ever had a sprained foot or stiff neck? If you sprained your foot, you should remember how tough it was for you to walk. You couldn't walk at the same speed and comfort you were accustomed to. If you had a stiff neck, you couldn't turn your head as easily and quickly as you normally would.

Some of us become a part of the body of Christ, but we can't play our part because we are like a sprained foot or stiff neck. We are attached to Christ, but we can't fully serve because we have sprained hearts, sprained minds and sprained souls. Like a sprained foot, we limit the ability of Christ's body to move and operate at full capacity. We can't put any pressure on a sprained foot without feeling the pain, which ultimately slows down our progress. When we are hurt, we can't handle any pain or pressure on our hearts, minds and souls when faced with a disappointment within the church or a disagreement with another church member. All of this slows down the movement of Christ in our lives and in the church.

Are you tired of slowing Christ down? Are you ready to become a useful part of His body? Are you ready to look beyond your pain and focus more on your healing? Are you ready to walk in and possess your blessings and experience a full life in Christ? If yes, you are ready to be taught, equipped and trained by an Apostle or a Pastor. It is the training and equipping from an Apostle or a Pastor that will take you to a higher level of living and power in Christ.

Knowing which part we play in the church is only the first step in becoming prepared for works of service. Next, we must look at the truth that as a member of the body of Christ, we are also the temple of the Holy Spirit. Looking at **1 Corinthians 6:19-20,** it says,

Do you not know that your body is a temple of the Holy Spirit, who is in you, whom you have received from God? You are not your own; you were bought at a price. Therefore honor God with your body.

Our bodies are a temple of the Holy Spirit. The word temple means sanctuary or shrine. This scripture doesn't mean that an individual is the temple of the Holy Spirit. Paul is stressing that as a collective body of believers, we form the body of Christ. The presence and power of God shows up when the body is in agreement, harmony and unity. The key point here to remember is that the Spirit of God lives in the church as it functions in unity with all members of the church.

We must do everything to make sure we don't grumble, argue and dislike each other in the local body that Christ has called us to serve in. When we argue and get mad at the Apostle or Pastor, we immediately block the flow, presence and power of God. We block God's power not only in our lives but in the lives of all the other people who are called to serve in that local church. We must be prayerful and forgiving of others who offend us and work to maintain love and unity at all times.

We must do everything to make sure we don't grumble, argue and dislike each other in the local body that Christ has called us to serve in. When we argue and get mad at the Apostle or Pastor, we immediately block the flow, presence and power of God.

---

1 Corinthians 6:19-20 says,

Do you not know that your body is a temple of the Holy Spirit, who is in you, whom you have received from God? <u>You are not your own;</u> you were bought at a price. Therefore honor God with your body.

It is important to remember that we are not our own. In other words, as a part of the body of Christ, we are not free to operate on our own. We must operate within the context and direction of the local body where we worship and serve. We will not be blessed independently of the body of believers. In other words, as a part of the local church we serve in and worship, we are blessed as others are blessed and judged as others are judged. This is why it's important to pray about any church we want to join. We must pray to be sure that the Holy Spirit is truly leading us to that church. The Holy Spirit will choose and lead us to a local body (church) where we will grow, prosper and be blessed. Our success is based on how we operate in the unique gifting that He has assigned to us. Once we accept the training and teaching of leadership from the Apostle or Pastor, we will begin to walk in our purpose and build up our local church.

We must never forget that we **<u>are not our own</u>.** We don't operate independently of others in our local church. We operate in accordance with how they operate. All of our blessings hinge on the obedience and roles that others play in the body of Christ at our local church. Now, we can understand the role of satan in the body of Christ. He comes to kill, steal, destroy and cause division. Once he does his work, he can sit back and relax. He knows that God can't move in a divided and hateful body. Satan's work is to get us to a point where we can't get along with anyone. His goal is for us to get frustrated within our church until we become disengaged and end up at home alone, having church by ourselves.

> *We don't operate independently of others in our local church.*
>
> *We operate in accordance with how they operate.*

We must be mindful that having church at home by ourselves will not produce the blessings of God because it is contradictory to God's purpose for establishing the church. The church was established so that all believers come together in unity and accomplish more than they could by themselves. That is why we have all been given a unique gifting — when put together with the gifts of others in our local church, we can accomplish great things in Christ Jesus. It is important that we work hard to maintain unity, love and peace in our local church. We are not our own! We can't operate on our own. We can't even get blessed on our own. We are blessed together, disciplined together, trained together and empowered together.

Below, write down the names of people you have experienced some problems with at your local church. Next, write down the problem. Then, list how you plan to bring peace and unity between you and each person. Lastly, write down how you might have contributed to the problem. Please make sure you list how you may have contributed to the problem. If you don't think you contributed to the problem at all, you are probably the one at fault the most in the relationship.

Name of each person

1. _____

2. _____

3. _____

4. _____

5. _____

The problem I have with each person is:

1. _____

2. _____

3. _____

4. _____

5. _____

I plan to do the following to resolve the problem I have with each person.

1. _____

2. _____

3. _____

4. _____

5. _____

I contributed to the problem I am having with each person by:

1. _____

2. _____

3. _____

4. _____

5. _____

Getting everyone at a local church to love each other, walk in peace together and operate in their unique gifts is not as easy as it sounds. In fact, scripture shows us just how difficult it is to achieve unity, peace and love in a local church. Look at **Ephesians 4:11-13** again:

It was he who gave some to be apostles, some to be prophets, some to be evangelists, and some to be pastors and teachers, to prepare God's people for works of service, so <u>that the body of Christ may be built up until we all reach unity in the faith</u> and in the knowledge of the Son of God <u>and become mature</u>, attaining to the whole measure of the fullness of Christ.

God wants the body of Christ to be built up. He wants it to be built up until it reaches unity. We will reach maturity as we get to know Christ and emulate Him in everything we do.

Christ was a servant. **Mark 10:45** shows us what Christ says about His attitude towards service to others. It says,

For even the Son of Man <u>did not come to be served, but to serve,</u> and to give his life as a ransom for many.

What a mature attitude to have. Christ Jesus said He came to serve and not be served. When we can reach a point in our Christian church lives where we realize that we are here to serve and not be served, we will have reached a level of maturity in the body of Christ that will bring blessings to all of us. To serve means to be an attendant and to wait on. That's right! We have been called to attend to others and wait upon others as God sees fit. The Holy Spirit will guide us to a local church and assign us to an Apostle or Pastor who will train and equip us in the ministry of serving by attending to the needs of others and waiting on them.

31

> *When we can reach a point in our Christian church lives where we realize that we are here to serve and not be served, we will have reached a level of maturity in the body of Christ that will bring blessings to all of us.*

Let's take a minute and examine our level of maturity. Babies depend on their caregivers to feed, clean and provide everything for them. A caregiver knows when a baby is hungry because the baby might cry. A caregiver also knows when a baby needs to be changed because the baby might smell or cry loudly. A caregiver can even figure out when a baby needs something because the baby may become very fussy and loud — even to the point of screaming and pitching a fit. Babies depend on someone else to take care of all their needs. As parents or caregivers, we will wait on our little children constantly and never expect anything in return from them at their young age. We know they are too young to do anything on their own or for anyone else. However, as they get older, going from one or two years old to about seven or eight years old, we expect them to be able to do certain things for themselves, like feed themselves with a fork and knife. We expect them to go to the bathroom on their own and clean up after themselves.

As they reach 17 or 18 years old, we expect them to now go beyond taking care of themselves to handling certain tasks and taking on the responsibilities of doing things for us as parents or caregivers as well. We expect them to go to the store and get things for us, clean up certain parts of the house and even cut the lawn on a regular basis. These are things we expect them to do only as they mature.

The way we expect our children to serve the family unit as they mature, God expects the same service from us as we mature in Christ. We may come to church crying, messed up and complaining. We may come hurting and yelling. We may even come pitching a fit. However, Christ expects us to get to a level of maturity where we go from crying to helping others dry their tears. He wants us to wait on others by helping them clean up their messed up lives. The point here is that we have not reached a level of maturity in the body of Christ until we are helping others who are new in Christ. When we can serve the local church by helping others, we have reached a level of maturity. Being mature allows us to walk in the fullness of Christ where blessings flow.

Complete the following exercises to find out your level of maturity in Christ.

1. When I first came to Christ in the year _____, I was experiencing the following challenges in my life:

   _____

   _____

   _____

2. I (check one) _____ *still* or _____ *no longer* face the challenges I had when I first became a Christian.

3. Below are the reasons why I do or don't have the same challenges in my life that I faced when I first became a Christian.

   _____

   _____

   _____

After completing the exercise, how do you rate your maturity in Christ right now? Have you overcome the challenges that you had to face when you first became a Christian? Are you still dealing with those same challenges? Before we deal with your first response, let's look at how you responded to the second and third statements. If you checked "still" on the second statement, then you haven't matured to a new level in Christ since first coming to Him. If you checked "no longer," you have matured in

Christ. If you listed reasons why you do have the same challenges, you must face the fact that you have a lot of work to do. You should also realize that while you have been attached to the body of Christ through your local church, you have not been actively engaged in your local church by serving and helping your Apostle or Pastor. Did this statement make you upset? Are you puzzled by this statement? If so, think about this truth: There is no record in scripture that shows Peter, Paul, Matthew, Mark, Timothy or others constantly dealing with the same problem or trouble. The few times they encountered any challenges, they presented them to God and kept working for Him in spite of what they were dealing with. As a result, they moved on to bigger and better things in Christ versus dwelling on the same old issues.

How often have you let a problem or circumstance stop you from going to church? How often has someone who hurt your feelings stopped you from going to church? Finally, how often has someone let you down in your local church, you couldn't get over it and decided to leave the church? If you can relate to these examples, think now about the impact this may have had on your personal life. Since then, how many blessings have you received? How long has it been since you experienced a blessing? Think about this for a moment. There may be a connection between not being involved in your local church and the blessings you receive.

Again, satan and his demonic influences will cause us to stop attending and being involved in the body of Christ. Once we fall victim to satan's scheme of separating us from the church, we then become weak and vulnerable to depression, guilt, fear and eventually begin to live less than a full life. **John 10:10** reinforces this truth by showing us that,

The thief comes only to steal and kill and destroy; I have come that they <u>may have life,</u> and <u>have it to the full.</u>

Being an active part of the body of Christ gives us a full life. Satan, the thief, comes in the church and causes confusion that robs us of a full life in Christ. A full life is connected to the body of Christ in the local church serving alongside an Apostle or a Pastor. There are many saved Christians, who still live an empty life while here on earth. Why? They are not serving in the body of Christ, and as a result, they have no power, blessings and authority to walk in a full life.

A full life is connected to the body of Christ in the local church serving alongside an Apostle or a Pastor.

Now let's conclude this chapter by taking a final look at **Ephesians 4:11-12:**

36

It was he who gave some to be <u>apostles,</u> some to be prophets, some to be evangelists, and some to be <u>pastors</u> and teachers, <u>to prepare God's people for works of service,</u> so that the body of Christ may be built up until we all reach unity in the faith and in the knowledge of the Son of God and become mature, attaining to the whole measure of the fullness of Christ.

Remember that the word prepare means, complete furnishing or the perfecting of a person. The perfecting or complete furnishing we should experience can't come unless an Apostle, a Pastor or one of the other three people who serve in the five-fold ministry of the body of Christ is placed in our lives. We can't benefit from this training and equipping until we give our lives to Christ and become a part of the body of Christ by joining a local church. Once we are a part of His body, we must remember that we are also a temple of the Holy Spirit. As a temple of the Holy Spirit, we must work to keep the house united by forgiving each other when we are offended or hurt.

God will only dwell and manifest His presence in us after we are fully furnished. Do you see it yet? Do you? Only as we are being perfected in the body of Christ, can we expect to see His glory and experience His blessings that He has for us. Thank God for our spiritual leaders. They hold the key to us becoming more than a house, but a house completely furnished with everything we need. What a blessing it is to know that serving with and being under an Apostle or a Pastor prepares us for a full life in Christ right now! We don't have to let problems and troubles reign in our lives. We can present them to Christ and continue serving in the local church we are assigned to by the Holy Spirit and walk in an abundance of blessings every day. What a blessing it is to know this.

Are you ready to serve in your local church? Are you ready for a better life? Are you ready to possess the power of God in your daily life? If so, unlock and release your blessings by serving with your Apostle and Pastor at your local church today. Don't waste any more time. God is waiting on us to wait on someone else. Once we wait on others, He will wait on us. He will bless us above our wildest imagination.

Chapter 2 Review and Exercise

1. The church is the body of Christ. When we accept Jesus Christ into our lives, become a believer of Christ and join a church, we become a part of His body.

2. In order for a body to operate, all parts must function correctly or the body is not able to operate at 100% capacity.

3. We must do everything to make sure we don't grumble, argue and dislike each other in the local body that Christ has called us to serve in. When we argue and get mad at the Apostle or Pastor, we immediately block the flow, presence and power of God.

4. We don't operate independently of others in our local church. We operate in accordance with how they operate.

5. When we can reach a point in our Christian church lives where we realize that we are here to serve and not be served, we will have reached a level of maturity in the body of Christ that will bring blessings to all of us.

6. A full life is connected to the body of Christ in the local church serving alongside an Apostle or a Pastor.

Spiritual Exercise

1. Write down the key things you have learned from this chapter.

   _____

   _____

   _____

   _____

   _____

2. Write a prayer to the Lord to help you develop a heart for your Apostle or Pastor.

   _____

   _____

   _____

   _____

   _____

Chapter 3

Serve With Your Heart, Not Just With Your Hands

Whatever you do, work at it with all your heart, as working for the Lord, not for men, since you know that you will receive an inheritance from the Lord as a reward. It is the Lord Christ you are serving.

Colossians 3:23-24

If we take a look at Colossians 3:23-24, we see that God wants us to work with our hearts, not just our hands. It is easy to be given an assignment in ministry and just run off and do the assignment. However, we must realize that just doing what we are asked to do is not enough. That's right! Just completing a task assigned by our Apostle or Pastor does not bring rewards from God to us. We must have an attitude of dedication, commitment and excellence that can only come from our heart. When we serve with dedication, commitment and excellence, scripture says we are rewarded from heaven by God Almighty. And in order to be rewarded by God, we must put our heart into our service.

41

> *We must have an attitude of dedication, commitment and excellence that can only come from our heart.*

Do you put your heart into your work in ministry? Or, do you just do enough to get the assignment done? Do you dread serving in a particular ministry at your local church? You must honestly think about these questions to see if you are putting your heart into your assignments given by God.

When you go to your church and get ready to serve in your assigned ministry, how do you feel?

_____

_____

_____

What do you think about the feelings you experience before you serve each Sunday or any other day? What do you think these feelings mean?

_____

_____

_____

Let's begin to take a look at these responses and try to work on a strategy for us to become excited or maintain excitement about our ministry assignments. The key to our continued blessings from God is to be able to work in our ministry assignments with an engaged heart. We simply have to put our hearts into what we do. If our hearts aren't into what we do, we can't give our best effort where we are called to serve. We must learn how to give our best. And giving our best can't happen if our hearts aren't into what we do.

> *The key to our continued blessings from God is to be able to work in our ministry assignments with an engaged heart.*

When we put our heart into service, we are dedicated, committed and will produce excellence in any task. We hear everyone talk about excellence. Excellence in ministry has to be one of the biggest buzz words ever used in churches across the country for the past 15 years. However, excellence is a process not an isolated trait. To understand how achieving excellence in ministry is part of a process, when we are given an assignment or position in ministry, we must:

*1. Become **dedicated**.*

*2. Become **committed**.*

*3. Operate in **excellence**.*

There is a difference between being dedicated, committed and excellent. Dedication means that at the beginning of an assignment, we pray to God and become consecrated toward the completion of the project, assignment or position. We make it special. We make it holy. We make a vow to God that everything the Holy Spirit has poured into us will now be used to complete our assignment. We may even participate in a church-wide dedication ceremony in which the Apostle or Pastor anoints and empowers us for this sacred and holy purpose of God. We may even have to stand before our congregation as we are anointed.

After we become dedicated, we must then become committed toward the completion of our assignment. We must be careful to remember that the word commitment doesn't mean what we will do or hope to do. No! The word commitment means that the work we agree to complete will be done. It means that it is already in the process toward completion. The word commitment means that nothing will stop this from happening. For example, no argument with another church member will stop our assignment from being completed. It means no member can hurt our feelings and make us drop out of church and not complete the assignment. It means that we won't get mad with the Apostle or Pastor of our church and leave without completing our assignment when we don't understand everything that is going on about certain church matters. Commitment means we agree and make a vow to get things done no matter what. Commitment also means to become engaged and involved in the assignment. Engagement and involvement means that we are actively aware and process all that we must do to make our assignment a first class finished product.

We need to make a special note to ourselves that doing something or performing a task doesn't mean we are engaged and involved with that task. Let's use driving a car to work every day as an example. Most of us drive to work every day. We usually take the same route. We pass the same road signs, traffic lights and buildings. Yet, if we were asked how long in minutes and seconds we spend at a particular traffic light, we couldn't specifically answer that question. Or, how many buildings there are from one exit to the next exit, we couldn't answer that one either. How about what is the actual distance between each exit? Again, we may give an answer but it would probably be wrong as well. Why can't we answer these questions? Shouldn't we be able to rattle off the correct answers quickly? Think about it.

45

Most of us drive to work more often than we do anything else. Some of us drive to and from work two times a day, five days a week. That is 500 times a year that we go to and from the same place. Shouldn't we know the details of each trip? Shouldn't we know every little detail along the way? Well, the reason we don't is because we are not engaged or involved in our commute. We are simply going through the motions. Yes, there are a few signs, buildings, etc. we will remember, but we will most likely not be able to give the details of the entire trip. It is alarming, but most of us are very passive, non-engaged drivers. Now that we have cell phones and texting capabilities, we really can't stay focused on the task at hand, which is to get to work safely and watch for other drivers. Believe it or not, simply turning on the radio or listening to a CD takes our focus off of the task at hand, which is to drive defensively and safely. From this example, we learn that to be engaged and involved requires all of our energy, thoughts and physical abilities to be aware, alert and receptive to everything around us.

Are you in a ministry now at your church where you are just going through the motions? Do you work in Audio/Video (A/V) sales, sit behind the table or counter, and if members or guests ask to buy something, you sell them what they ask for and that's the end of it? Can you even remember what they bought? Or more importantly, can you remember what products in the

A/V ministry sold the most or were most requested for each service you volunteered? Are you on the Intercessory Prayer team? Do you get to church just in time before each prayer session, pray and then that's the end of it? In other words, can you remember all of the prayers? Do you have to be told to improve things in your ministry? Is the Apostle or Pastor you serve with consistently asking you to come up with new ideas? Sadly, is the Apostle or Pastor you serve with always the one coming up with the new ideas for your ministry?

The answers to these questions should have made most of us aware that we might not be as engaged or involved in ministry as we should be. We are simply going through the motions. We are simply doing enough to say we did something. *We must remember that doing something is doing nothing when it doesn't produce our best.* Doing anything in order to do something will only produce a mess. However, doing our best at everything means anything we do or produce will be blessed. To do our best, we must give our best. To give our best we must be engaged and involved.

We must remember that doing something is doing nothing when it doesn't produce our best.

Once we become dedicated and committed, we are now ready to operate in excellence. Excellence means to go beyond, have high standards, produce works of distinction and have high expectations for end results. There is no way we can expect to operate in excellence without dedication and commitment. Excellence is the product and fruit of dedication and commitment. If an organization has people on a particular assignment who are not dedicated and committed, excellence will never happen. We are operating in excellence when we don't have to be told what to do, reminded of what we need to do or even be evaluated on how good we do something. NO! **Excellence is going above what is expected to be done!** It's when we can do something or complete something and redefine how it should be done. When we set new standards for what people expect to receive from us, we are walking in excellence.

How can we redefine quality, excellence, service, professionalism and hospitality to members and guests who come to our church every service if the leaders who are serving don't have an ounce of these qualities in their character? The answer is: we can't. It is impossible. It will never happen. Interestingly, when people come to the house of God, they should see excellence at a level they can't articulate. Starbucks, Wal-Mart and Carnival Cruise Lines should not be the first names that fall off the lips of people when they think of excellent service. The local church in their community should be the first name that they recite. We should focus on making the worship experience as a model for Fortune 500 CEOs to come and learn how to implement for their companies. However, this kind of service will never happen until we have heart-engaged leaders reaching the hearts of members and guests who come to our churches.

The church must look for the right heart-engaged people to lead and work in ministries. When people can see that our hearts are engaged in what we do, their hearts will desire what we do. People desire to see God. But, they want to see an excellent, organized and loving God. They want to see God every time they walk in our church. They want to see God when they drive into the parking lot, walk into the guest reception area, and drop off their children at the nursery. People want to see God when they talk to ministry staff members, participate in the worship service, watch the praise and worship team, listen to the choir, and hear the sermon. They want to see God when they receive help from the hosts or ushers and interact with everyone in a leadership position. They don't want to see complainers working at the front door. They don't want to see ushers who are crying because Deacon Buddy hurt their feelings earlier that day. No! They want to see God through leaders who operate in unity and love despite hurts and pains that may develop from working in ministry and with each other.

> ***When people can see that our hearts are engaged in what we do, their hearts will desire what we do.***

We must have leaders who are dedicated, committed and ready to operate in excellence. We all must work to have these three servant traits in order to be blessed and rewarded by God. In fact, it is when we possess these three traits we earn the right to be called a ***"Heart-Engaged Servant."***

<u>**Three Traits of a Heart-Engaged Servant That Brings Blessings**</u>

Excellence (to go above and beyond, high standards/expectations, distinctive service)

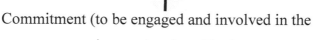

Commitment (to be engaged and involved in the assignment and position)

Dedication (to reverence the assignment or position and make it a sacred, holy purpose for God)

Below, write how you plan to become more **dedicated** to the ministry you serve in at your local church.

_____

_____

_____

Next, write how you plan to become **committed** to the ministry you serve in at your local church.

_____

_____

_____

Finally, write how you plan to operate in **excellence** in the ministry you serve in at your local church.

_____

_____

_____

Our ability to engage our hearts in the assignments given to us by our Apostle or Pastor is the key to receiving our blessings from God. We must be careful to make sure we stay engaged and involved in what we are doing at all times. We must learn to think above and beyond our ministry. Thinking above and beyond our ministry means we are always looking for new ways to redefine and deliver excellence to the people God has called us to serve. Our Apostle or Pastor should always cherish and celebrate our ability to advance and improve our ministries. Our Apostle or Pastor should not have to always push us or remind us of things to do in our ministries. We should keep a pipeline of new ideas flowing into our ministries at all times. If we do these things, we will be serving God while pleasing our Apostle or Pastor as he or she watches us get blessed and go to new levels in the body of Christ, which is His church.

> *Our ability to engage our hearts in the assignments given to us by our Apostle or Pastor is the key to receiving our blessings from God.*

Chapter 3 Review and Exercise

1. We must have an attitude of dedication, commitment and excellence that can only come from our heart.

2. The key to our continued blessings from God is to be able to work in our ministry assignments with an engaged heart.

3. When we are given an assignment or position in ministry, we must become dedicated, become committed and operate in excellence.

4. We must remember that doing something is doing nothing when it doesn't produce our best.

5. When people can see that our hearts are engaged in what we do, their hearts will desire what we do.

6. Our ability to engage our hearts in the assignments given to us by our Apostle or Pastor is the key to receiving our blessings from God.

Spiritual Exercise

1. Write down the key things you have learned from this chapter.

   _____

   _____

   _____

   _____

   _____

2. Write a prayer to the Lord to help you become committed, dedicated and operate in excellence.

   _____

   _____

   _____

   _____

   _____

Chapter 4

Obedience to Leaders:
The Key to Blessings

Obey your leaders and submit to their authority. They keep watch over you as men who must give an account. Obey them so that their work will be a joy, not a burden, for that would be of no advantage to you.

Hebrews 13:17

Many Christians who serve in ministry at their local church use **Colossians 3:23** as their favorite scripture for rebelling against their church leaders. Let's take a look:

Whatever you do, work at it with all your heart, as working for the Lord, not for men...

But as we examine this scripture closely, we see how "working for the Lord, not for men" can take on a different meaning. Here's an example. We join a church. We find work to do, or we are assigned a task. We work with all of our heart. Then, something happens. As soon as things don't go the way we thought they would or should, we begin to automatically start working for the Lord, not for men. Did you get that? We make up our minds, based on scripture, that we are no longer serving our church leaders. We are only serving God. Does that make any sense? In other words, we begin to bypass our church leaders and not submit to their authority. When we are asked by our leaders to do something we don't like or feel comfortable doing, we start working for the Lord, not for men. Interestingly, even when we decide we just don't feel like doing something, we start working for the Lord, not for men. However, we must begin to look at this scripture and ask ourselves if this is the meaning God intended when He spoke these words through Paul.

Many members of a local church use Colossians 3:23 to develop a rebellious attitude toward the leaders at their local church. They look at this scripture and think that it gives them the right to question the authority of the leaders. Some church members look at Colossians 3:23 and begin to think they have the right to question everything that their leaders ask them to do. When some members are asked to do something, they may even tell the leaders that they must wait to hear from God before they agree to do it. Is this right? Is this the attitude we are to take while serving in ministry? Is this kind of response to leadership biblical?

Let's look at Hebrews 13:17 and see what scripture has to say. **Hebrews 13:17** clearly states:

Obey your leaders and submit to their authority. They keep watch over you as men who must give an account. Obey them so that their work will be a joy, not a burden, for that would be of no advantage to you.

Wow! These are Godly statements for us to follow. God wants us to be at a place of obedience when it comes to our response to the leaders who have been placed over us in the local church. Notably, we are required not only to be obedient according to Hebrews 13:17, but we also are instructed to be submissive to the leaders who have been placed over us. We must grasp the truth that as we serve, obey and submit to our leaders, we are serving, obeying and submitting to God. We must grasp this truth to be blessed by God. We serve God by serving under the leaders who have been placed over us. We work for God as we demonstrate love, obedience and submission to the leadership at our local church.

We must grasp the truth that as we serve, obey and submit to our leaders, we are serving, obeying and submitting to God.

Process of Releasing God's Blessing in Our Lives Through Service in Ministry

Step 1: God moves on the leader's heart to ask us to do something in ministry.

↓

Step 2: God watches to see if we will serve and be obedient, submissive and loving by doing what the ministry leader asks us to do.

↓

Step 3: God observes to see if we approach our ministry assignment with our whole heart. He checks to see if we work for the leader as if we are working for Him directly.

↓

Step 4: As we complete our assignments, we show God that we trust Him and respect the authority of the leader He placed over us.

↓

Step 5: We are then blessed by God as we serve our church leader as if we are working for God Himself.

Also notice that if we are obedient and submissive to leaders in our church, we are at an advantage. What advantage is the scripture talking about? Well, the advantage is being able to receive the blessings of God in our lives as we serve and make the leaders placed over us experience joy. Not only are we to cultivate joy for our leaders, we are to not be a burden to them as well.

The key to understanding **Colossians 3:23: Whatever you do, work at it with all your heart, as working for the Lord, not for men...** is hidden in the simple word, "as." The scripture says work at it with all your heart, **AS.** We must look deeper into the word "*as*." In Colossians 3:23, "as" is used as an adjective which means, to the same degree, amount or extent; similarly or equally. God is telling Paul to tell the workers in the church to not consider work as something they do for a man. The work they do should be approached with the reverence and respect they give God. In other words, what this means for us is we shouldn't do our work half heartedly.

We should put our whole heart into our work as if we are working for God Himself. Truth be told, we should picture God speaking to us when a church leader is asking us to do something. Our devotion, dedication and commitment should have the same sense of urgency that we would give God if He were there Himself. Again, He is there when we are serving in the church. He is looking to see if we are serving with whole-hearted devotion. So, we must serve our church leaders as if God is the one giving us the assignment. We should give our all, wholeheartedly to make sure our assignments are not just completed, but completed with excellence and love.

> *We should put our whole heart into our work as if we are*
> *working for God Himself. Truth be told, we should picture*
> *God speaking to us when a church leader is*
> *asking us to do something.*

Let's revisit **Hebrews 13:17** once again.

Obey your leaders and submit to their authority. They keep watch over you as <u>men who must give an account. Obey them so that their work will be a joy, not a burden,</u> for that would be of no advantage to you.

Do you see a powerful truth here? We must realize that Apostles and Pastors are required by God to give an account of how the members who are assigned to them are doing. Apostles and Pastors must report to God how we are maturing based on if we are serving with an obedient, submissive and loving heart in the church. Apostles and Pastors must pray and give an account to God. We should think of it as a job performance review. That's right! We go through a job performance review every time we serve in ministry. God is attentive to the kind of prayers Apostles and Pastors lift up to see how we are progressing toward being an active and productive part of the body of Christ.

> *We must realize that Apostles and Pastors are required by God to give an account of how the members who are assigned to them are doing.*

There is one main thing God doesn't want to be reported to Him by church leaders, and that is that we are a burden. God wants us to be obedient, submissive, joyful and loving. He doesn't want us to be a burden. The Greek definition of the word burden means to sigh, murmur, have grief and groan. This Greek meaning of burden means something different than how we define it today. To be a burden in ministry means that when we are given an assignment by a church leader, instead of being joyful, enthusiastic and full of vigor, we immediately sigh, murmur, display grief and groan. We have a very heavy and negative heart about what God wants to do through us, and we reject His Lordship in our lives.

In fact, sighing, murmuring, displaying grief and groaning are four things that God doesn't like. The Bible is full of examples of how He dealt with people who did such things. When we sigh, murmur, have grief and groan, we are not doing these things toward the leaders only; we are doing them toward God. For example, in **Exodus 16:8 (KJV)** we see that the murmurs against Moses were actually against God.

61

And Moses said, *This shall be,* **when the LORD shall give you in the evening flesh to eat, and in the morning bread to the full; for that the <u>LORD heareth your murmurings which ye murmur against him:</u> and what** *are* **we? <u>Your murmurings are not against us, but against the LORD.</u>**

> *When we sigh, murmur, have grief and groan,*
>
> *we are not doing these things toward the leaders only; we are*
>
> *doing them to God.*

The Israelites complained and murmured so much to Moses that he talked to God and gave a report about the behavior of the people to Him. Many times Moses covered for the people, but they murmured, whined, complained and sighed so much that he told God everything about them. Let's look at how God dealt with them. **Numbers 14:27-35 (KJV)** describes Moses' frustration and the result of the disobedience of the people:

<u>**How long** *shall I bear with* **this evil congregation, which murmur against me?**</u> **I have heard the murmurings of the children of Israel, which they murmur against me. Say unto them,** *As truly as* **I live, saith the LORD, as ye have spoken in mine ears, so will I do to you: Your carcases shall fall in this wilderness; and all that were numbered of you, according to your whole number, from twenty years old and upward,**

which have murmured against me, <u>Doubtless ye shall not</u> <u>come into the land,</u> *concerning* which I sware to make you dwell therein, save Caleb the son of Jephunneh, and Joshua the son of Nun. But your little ones, which ye said should be a prey, them will I bring in, and they shall know the land which ye have despised. But *as for* you, your carcases, they shall fall in this wilderness. And your children shall wander in the wilderness forty years, and bear your whoredoms, until your carcases be wasted in the wilderness. After the number of the days in which ye searched the land, *even* forty days, each day for a year, shall ye bear your iniquities, *even* forty years, and ye shall know my breach of promise. I the LORD have said, <u>I will surely do it unto all this evil</u> <u>congregation, that are gathered together against me: in this</u> <u>wilderness they shall be consumed, and there they shall die.</u>

Notice that God defines a church that murmurs as an evil church. That's right! When we become a burden to the leaders in our church, God views that church as evil. He then takes away blessings from us, and we wander in a state of bewilderment for a long period of time. See, when a church doesn't support its Apostle or Pastor, God acts against that church, and He dries up the blessings in it. While we may not be wandering around in an actual wilderness, we may be experiencing a drying up of His blessings, promises and closeness. We may not physically die when we murmur, but isn't it interesting how many of our dreams are dying?

Are you experiencing a dry and dying time in your life? Do you feel like you come to church and leave not satisfied? Does it seem like your life is going nowhere lately? If so, you may be going through a spiritual wilderness called on by God that will never get any better until you roll up your sleeves and stop sighing, murmuring, displaying grief and groaning. When we make a commitment to serve without complaining, He refreshes us and spiritually revives us in a very powerful way.

There are four things that kill a ministry: sighing, murmuring, displaying grief and groaning. Another way to define them would be to call them **ministry killers**. Sighing, murmuring, displaying grief and groaning will kill the spiritual life of a church and all who are a part of that church. We must never forget that we are all one body in Christ. When one person doesn't live up to what God calls him or her to be, the entire church begins a slow wilderness experience where we slowly dry up and spiritually die. We can resurrect our spiritual vigor as we make a commitment to rededicate ourselves through obedience, submission, love and a joyful heart. When we do, God will come into our lives with so much power we won't know how to act.

And if there are four ministry killers, there are also four things that resurrect a ministry: Obedience, submission, love and a joyful heart. If we exercise these four ways to resurrect ministry, our church will experience a powerful move of life where we can't contain the goodness of God.

Four Ministry Killers	**Four Ways to Resurrect Ministry**
1. Sighing	1. Obedience
2. Murmuring	2. Submission
3. Displaying Grief	3. Love
4. Groaning	4. Joyful Heart

There are four things that kill a ministry: sighing, murmuring, displaying grief and groaning. And, if there are four ministry killers, there are also four things that resurrect a ministry: Obedience, submission, love and a joyful heart.

Take a few moments and write how your attitude has been toward the leaders in your church lately.

_____

_____

_____

Write below how you plan to change your attitude toward the leaders in your church starting now.

_____

_____

_____

Take time and write a prayer to God and ask Him to forgive you if you know that you have not served your Apostle, Pastor or church leader the way scripture says you should serve.

_____

_____

_____

Chapter 4 Review and Exercise

1. We must grasp the truth that as we serve, obey and submit to our leaders, we are serving, obeying and submitting to God.

2. We should put our whole heart into our work as if we are working for God Himself. Truth be told, we should picture God speaking to us when a church leader is asking us to do something.

3. We must realize that Apostles and Pastors are required by God to give an account of how the members who are assigned to them are doing.

4. When we sigh, murmur, have grief and groan, we are not doing these things toward the leaders only; we are doing them to God.

5. There are four things that kill a ministry: sighing, murmuring, displaying grief and groaning. And, if there are four ministry killers, there are also four things that resurrect a ministry: Obedience, submission, love and a joyful heart.

Spiritual Exercise

1. Write down the key things you have learned from this chapter.

    _____

    _____

    _____

    _____

    _____

2. Write a prayer to the Lord to help you serve with obedience, submission, love and a joyful heart.

    _____

    _____

    _____

    _____

    _____

Chapter 5

Get Ready to Come Up in Ministry

The Lord descended to the top of Mount Sinai and <u>called</u>
<u>Moses to the top of the mountain</u>. So Moses went up.
Exodus 19:20

Moses said to the Lord, <u>"The people cannot come up</u> Mount
Sinai, because you yourself warned us, 'Put limits around the
mountain and set it apart as holy.' The Lord replied, "Go down
and bring Aaron up with you. But the priests and the people
must not force their way through to come up to the Lord, or he
will break out against them."
Exodus 19:23-24

One of the greatest things that can happen to us in ministry is
when our Apostle or Pastor raises us up to a new level of
responsibility. In Exodus chapter 19, we see God is talking to
Moses. He is about to share something very special and secretive
with him. He is about to share the Ten Commandments.
However, God wants Moses to allow Aaron to hear His divine
charge for all humans on earth. We also must note that it wasn't
Moses' idea to bring Aaron up, it was God's command. We must

never forget that when God's leader calls you up to a new assignment, it is because God called the leader to call you up. How many times has a church leader talked to you about a new position in ministry, and you said no? How many times have you second guessed your Apostle or Pastor when he or she told you to get ready for a new, higher assignment in the church? How many times have you hesitated to move forward in a new ministry assignment that you have been called up to serve in the local church?

We must never forget that when God's leader calls you up to a new assignment, it is because God called the leader to call you up.

We can all identify with making a decision to receive a new assignment that required more responsibility and time commitments in the church. However, we must never forget that it is God who is calling us to the new assignment. He is just speaking through our church leader. Notice **Exodus 19:20** says that,

The Lord descended to the top of Mount Sinai and <u>called Moses to the top</u> of the mountain. So Moses went up.

Here we see God's leader being summoned to the top. Do you see it? Do you see that God's leader is at the top? The top is a very high place where only a few people can go, can survive and are invited. That's right! God sent an invitation to His leader, Moses. He responded quickly and with great expectancy. God wants to share something very sacred and special with His leader. However, God knows that what He is about to share is too much for any one man to carry alone. God knows that the responsibility that is about to be given to Moses must be carried and shared with someone else. He then tells Moses to summon Aaron. Aaron has been summoned to go to a higher level with his Pastor, Moses, to Mount Sinai where others are forbidden to go.

We should not feel bad when we are not allowed to know God's plan for certain things that are happening in the church, such as business operations and ministry reassignments. We are not given this knowledge because God has ordained only certain people to know His plan for the church. He has equipped these few leaders to carry and execute His plan flawlessly. The worst thing that could ever happen to us is to overhear a plan of God and become so overwhelmed by it that we quit the church. We are overwhelmed because we know we can't fulfill the requirements needed to complete the task. We must remember that God wants to bring up certain people in ministry according to the ability that He has given them.

Process of God's Calling In Ministry

God chooses who He wants on certain assignments

God calls the leader up to a sacred place

God tells His leader who to bring up to serve

The leader summons the person

The person shares the responsibility of completing the assignments

---

We must remember that God wants to bring up certain people in ministry according to the ability that He has given them.

Now the question becomes, why did God choose Aaron out of all the other priests, Levites, Israelites and other servants? The answer is very simple. It was Aaron who was by Moses' side during the pronouncement of God's requests to Pharaoh. It was Aaron who spoke Moses' thoughts to Pharaoh. It was Aaron who lifted Moses' hand all day and night when the Israelites were fighting the Amalekites. It was Aaron who stood with Moses when the people were mad with Moses, Aaron and God and demanded water because they were thirsty. It was Aaron who took his staff and threw it down when Moses gave the command to do so — not knowing what would happen when he did.

Have you ever wondered how Aaron could have known what to say to Pharaoh while speaking for Moses in the midst of all the hostility of a famed king? How could he speak for Moses and not make a mistake? It is because he had Moses' heart. How could he hold up Moses' hand without quitting or becoming discouraged in the midst of a battle? How could he stand with Moses while facing an angry mob that demanded water because they were thirsty and ready to do anything to quench their thirst — including murder? How could Aaron throw down his staff at Moses' command and trust Moses that God would perform a miracle to counter Pharaoh's evil acts of divination? How could he be so dedicated and committed to supporting Moses without wavering? It is simple: He had Moses' heart. Watch this now! He didn't chase Moses down to get his heart. Moses chose Aaron and gave Aaron his heart.

In **Exodus 4:11-17,** it says

The Lord said to him, "Who gave man his mouth? Who makes him deaf or mute? Who gives him sight or makes him blind? Is it not I, the Lord? Now go; I will help you speak and will teach you what to say." But Moses said, "O Lord, please send someone else to do it." Then the Lord's anger burned against Moses and he said, "What about your brother, Aaron the Levite? I know he can speak well. <u>He is already on his way to meet you, and his heart will be glad when he sees you. You shall speak to him and put words in his mouth; I will help both of you speak and will teach you what to do. He will speak to the people for you, and it will be as if he were your mouth and as if you were God to him.</u> But take this staff in your hand so you can perform miraculous signs with it."

Moses admitted to God that he had doubts he could speak well enough to lead the people. God became angry with Moses and prepared Aaron to assist Moses in his duties. It is interesting: As Moses doubts his ability to speak well, Aaron is on his way up to meet him. Notice how God has moved on Aaron's heart to seek out Moses to assist him in his assignment from God. Notice how Moses doesn't get angry when Aaron shows up. Moses is happy and relieved to see that God chose Aaron to be by his side. It is at this point that Moses gives Aaron his heart.

When Apostles or Pastors accept someone God calls to help in the church, they give that person their heart. Notice also that the scripture says in **Exodus 4:14: He is already on his way to meet you, and his heart will be glad when he sees you.** Wow! What a great thing! Aaron comes toward Moses with a glad heart. In fact, God tells Moses that Aaron's heart will be glad when he sees Moses. This point is key to understand. Aaron's heart would not be glad **until** he sees Moses. This truth is something all Apostles or Pastors should look for in their local churches. They should look for people who become glad when they see their leader.

When Apostles or Pastors accept someone God calls to help in the church, they give that person their heart.

A leader can recognize the people who God has called to serve by watching their attitudes when they are in the leader's presence. How is your attitude when you see your Apostle, Pastor or church leader? Do you frown? Are you always down? Are you mad all the time? If you are, you could be disqualifying yourself from being elevated to a new level in ministry and God's blessings. Leaders look for happy people. Leaders look for joyous people. Leaders look for people who are glad to serve and help other people. The last thing the church needs today are mean, nasty, sad, gloom and doom types of attitudes. The church needs lively people who love serving others. Ministry service is not a place for upset, nasty, unforgiving and impolite people.

If people were to describe you and your attitude at church, what do you think they would say?

_____

_____

_____

How do you think your Apostle, Pastor or church leader would describe your attitude, facial expression, etc.?

_____

_____

_____

Write down if this disposition is how you want to be known in your church.

_____

_____

_____

Take a moment and write any changes to your demeanor and attitude you think you need to make, if any.

_____

_____

_____

Finally we must recognize the truth that there will be times when we will not be included in certain ministry assignments. We shouldn't feel like we are not good enough, are being picked on or looked down upon, or that someone doesn't like us. The truth is we may not have been called by God to be a part of that particular assignment.

Let's look again at **Exodus 19:24** where it says,

The Lord replied, "Go down and <u>bring Aaron up with you.</u> But the <u>priests and the people must not force their way through</u> to come up to the Lord, or <u>he will break out against them.</u>"

Wow! What an insightful scripture. We see here that Moses and Aaron have been called up to a higher level, but certain other people within the "congregation" are forbidden to try and get to the level that Moses and Aaron have been called to serve. God even tells Moses to warn the people to not try and force their way up to this higher assignment. Why do you think God says this? Is He a mean God? Is He prejudging others who want to serve? No! He knows that He chose these two men to complete a task for Him that He designed for them and only them to complete. He has given them certain abilities through the Holy Spirit to be able to perform the duties necessary to make the assignment successful. We must always remember that God will never require more of us than the ability He has already given us. God doesn't want us to force our will on Him to help Him. He wants us to watch and wait on Him and become a part of His plan when He is ready for us to serve with Him.

> *We must always remember that God will never require more of us than the ability He has already given us.*

Let's look at **John 5:19** where it says,

Jesus gave them this answer: "I tell you the truth, <u>the Son can do nothing by himself; he can do only what he sees his Father doing,</u> because whatever the Father does the Son also does.

Here we see Christ Jesus stating that He never places His will or actions above His Father's. He says that He waits, watches and replicates what He sees His Father doing. Why is this so? Christ

Jesus says I will never force my way in the way of the Father's work. Christ Jesus says that we should learn that when we force our way into God's work, we will mess things up and cause unnecessary trouble, burdens and discomfort in our lives.

Are you feeling heavily burdened in the ministry you are working in? Are you experiencing heartache where you placed yourself to serve in your ministry? Do you take your ill feelings at home with you after service and can't shake them for hours and days at a time? If you answered yes to any of these questions, here are a few more key questions to ask yourself. Did you force yourself into the ministry you are serving in, or were you called to it? Did a leader ask you to become a part of the ministry, or did you walk up to him or her and express your desire to become a part of the ministry? These are key questions you must ask yourself to help sort out what you might be experiencing.

True service in ministry is one where we are all blessed with no stress in the ministries we are called to serve. Please understand that when we are called to a ministry, we may feel very heavy and uncomfortable at first. However, our feelings have nothing to do with the long-term blessing we will experience when we are properly placed in a ministry that comes from a calling by our Apostle, Pastor or church leader. So we must make sure our calling is just that: a call and not a dial up.

> *Our feelings have nothing to do with the long-term blessing we will experience when we are properly placed in a ministry that comes from a calling by our Apostle, Pastor or church leader.*

God says we should not dial up our calling. We shouldn't dial up where we want to serve. We shouldn't dial up when we want to serve. Finally we shouldn't dial up who we want to serve under. God says if we start dialing up our own ministry callings, we most likely will be dialing up a mess. All we have to do is serve faithfully where we have been placed, as menial as the assignment may seem. Then one day we will get a higher calling that will bring a higher blessing.

> *One day we will get a higher calling that will bring a higher blessing.*

Aaron went from holding snakes to holding worship services. He went from holding up Moses' hand to holding up the Ten Commandments. He went from holding a rod that turned into a snake to holding sacred articles dedicated to God as sacrificial offerings. Look at how he went from menial responsibilities to the most important position in the congregation. He became the first High Priest of the Israelites on this earth. What a difference a calling makes when you wait on it and not dial it up!

Chapter 5 Review and Exercise

1. We must never forget that when God's leader calls you up to a new assignment, it is because God called the leader to call you up.

2. We must remember that God wants to bring up certain people in ministry according to the ability that He has given them.

3. When Apostles or Pastors accept someone God calls to help in the church, they give that person their heart.

4. We must always remember that God will never require more of us than the ability He has already given us.

5. Our feelings have nothing to do with the long-term blessing we will experience when we are properly placed in a ministry that comes from a calling by our Apostle, Pastor or church leader.

6. One day we will get a higher calling that will bring a higher blessing.

Spiritual Exercise

1. Write down the key things you have learned from this chapter.

   _____

   _____

   _____

   _____

   _____

2. Write a prayer to the Lord to help you receive your Apostle's or Pastor's heart.

   _____

   _____

   _____

   _____

   _____

Chapter 6

Press On Toward the Prize

... I press on toward the goal to win the prize for which God has called me heavenward in Christ Jesus.
Philippians 3:14

When we serve in a ministry at our local church, we must be careful not to become so busy doing ministry work that we forget what we are supposed to be doing. That's right! It is easy to get so caught up in our ministry tasks that we forget what we are really supposed to be doing. Ministries that are in the order of God always set objectives, goals, action plans and contingency plans. It is important to know that ministry is more than just helping people, praying for people and praising God. Ministry is also a business. There is a business side of ministry that we must walk in. Even Christ Jesus knew what He was doing had to be structured and ordered with business principles.

It is important to know that ministry is more than just helping people, praying for people and praising God.

Ministry is also a business.

Let's look at **Luke 2:49 (KJV)**:

And he said unto them, How is it that ye sought me? wist [know] ye not that I must be about my Father's business?

As we can see here, Christ Jesus knew He had to operate in ministry on the principles of business.

A business is an organized unit that sets out to achieve the mission it is called to accomplish. Now, if a business has a mission, it also must set goals in order to gauge its progress toward achieving the mission. Our ministries within the church should be the same way. In fact, we have to be careful that we don't confuse busyness with business! Busyness is when we are doing a lot of things that feel good, look good and sound good. However, if what we are doing does not support our mission or purpose of why we are in existence, it is busyness. If what we are doing is unorganized, out of order and randomly executed, we are operating in busyness. If we have a lot of people coming to church on Sunday, stumbling into the service and stumbling out, we are operating in busyness. If they can't really put their finger on what they learned that day, or how their life has changed for the better because of the service, we are operating in busyness.

Now, when we operate in business, we shout, praise God, worship on Sunday, and as we operate within our ministries, we stay in line with the mission God ordained for the church.

Every church should have a mission, a vision and a value statement. Take a look at the boxes below. You'll see that it's important for a church to know why it exists, what it needs to become and how it makes a difference each day. Ministries within the church should have objectives, goals, action plans and contingency plans that line up with the church's overall mission. Each ministry should define what it wants to accomplish, how it will measure that progress, how things will get done and how it will handle unplanned events.

Church Order
Mission – Purpose of existence
Vision – What we need to become
Value Statement – What those we serve mean to us and the difference we will make in their lives

Ministry Order
Objective – What do we want to accomplish
Goal – Measurable progress towards the mission
Action Plan – How we put the goals into action
Contingency Plan – How we handle unplanned events

We must never forget that ministry order must line up with church order. All the things we do in ministry must contribute to achieving the mission, vision and values of our church. If we are doing things contrary to that, we are out of order and not operating in our true calling as church leaders. As a church, we think if we just open the doors and have praise and worship and a great sermon where people get healed, saved and delivered, we have done and are doing what we were called to do. We fool ourselves into thinking that we are achieving the mission of the organization.

We must never forget that ministry order must line up with church order. All the things we do in ministry must contribute to achieving the mission, vision and values of our church.

Aren't we supposed to save souls? Aren't we supposed to praise the Lord? Aren't we supposed to heal the sick? Yes we are, but we are to go beyond the busyness of saving, praising the Lord and healing. We must get to the business of maximizing the number of people God has opened the door to heal, save and commune with. Do you see the importance of goals yet? Let's see how Christ Jesus viewed this in **Luke 13:31-33.**

At that time some Pharisees came to Jesus and said to him, "Leave this place and go somewhere else. Herod wants to kill

you." He replied, "Go tell that fox, 'I will drive out demons and heal people today and tomorrow, and on the third day I will reach my goal. In any case, I must keep going today and tomorrow and the next day — for surely no prophet can die outside Jerusalem!'

In verse 33, Christ knows the exact number of people He will heal and deliver from the devil. He also knows the exact number of days He has to do it. He is in line with God and in time with God. In other words, He is about His Father's business. He knows that to miss any people or stop one day too early will mess up what His Father is doing. To be off point and out of time is to miss the business of ministry. We should never confuse the blessing of ministry with the business of ministry. They go hand in hand but are not potent if they are out of the order of God.

Have you ever been in a ministry where the move of God is strong and everyone is having a great time in the Lord? However, as time goes on, you become bored, your mind wanders or you feel left out or confused in the midst of this great move of God? If you have ever experienced this, it is because you probably have been in the middle of a blessed experience that didn't have the order required to make it a life changing moment. Here is another example to think about. Have you ever participated in a hand laying service where people are falling out and in the presence of God? Then, all of a sudden, people start falling on top of each other and getting hurt? Or, maybe you have seen people falling out in a hand laying service, and there is no one to catch them and they fall flat on the floor and hurt themselves. If so, you have experienced a blessed moment that was out of order. Paul knew the importance of order. In **1 Corinthians 14:40**, he says,

But everything should be done in a fitting and orderly way.

We are called to have structure and order in all activities in the church. Structure and order are key ingredients to conducting a business of excellence in a way that can help the church achieve its mission. Why is it necessary to have statements like a mission, vision, value, etc.? Why is it necessary to have objectives, goals, action plans and contingency plans? Because if we don't, we may miss the glory of God and His blessings. <u>**We must stay in line with Him and in time with Him.**</u>

> *Structure and order are key ingredients to conducting a business of excellence in a way that can help the church achieve its mission.*

Let's look more closely at objectives. An objective is something we want to accomplish at the end of our task. In other words, an objective states what we want to have accomplished after what we are working on is over. Or, an objective may be in the form of a question like, why are we doing this assignment? What do we want to accomplish after this assignment is over? The objective keeps a ministry on point in achieving the overall mission of the church. If we ever want to do something in our ministries, we should check our objective statement to see if what we are supposed to be doing is achieving the church's mission, or if our assignment is just a form of busyness.

In addition to objectives, we are reminded by Paul in Philippians 3:14 that when we serve in ministry, we are also called to have goals. A goal is not something that we say we are going to do. A goal is not something we hope we can do. A goal is something that we set to measure our progress in achieving an objective that we established. The objective we set should be in line with the mission of the church. That's why it's important for goals to be measurable, attainable and feasible. Goals we set in ministry should have numbers so that we can measure our progress toward achieving the set objective.

Again, looking at **Luke 13:32** we see Christ with quantifiable and measurable goals. The scripture shows us,

91

He replied, "Go tell that fox, 'I will drive out demons and heal people today and tomorrow, and <u>on the third day I will reach my goal.</u>'

Please notice how Christ states what He has to do, which is His objective. Then, He measures His progress toward reaching that objective by stating His goal of three days of driving out demons and healing people. Once He meets His goal, then He would have successfully reached the objective of what His Father wants Him to do.

Think about what would have happened if Jesus stopped on the second day. What might have happened if He stopped on the first day? Even more interesting, let's think about what would have happened if He didn't stop until the fourth day. If He had stopped the first or second day, He would have done great things but missed all the people who the Father wanted to deliver and heal. If He kept delivering and healing people on the fourth day, He would have been out of the will of the Father. Yes! That's right. He would have been doing a good thing but not a God ordained thing.

We must learn that even though we have the ability to operate in the power of God through the Holy Spirit, we should always make sure we are in God's will by being in His perfect timing. John makes this point clear. In **John 5:19** Jesus says,

"I tell you the truth, the Son can do nothing by himself; he can do only what he sees his Father doing, because whatever the Father does the Son also does."

Christ is saying that if He does anything on His own without His Father's approval, He knows He is out of God's will and operating on His own. We should never forget that Christ never operated in His ministry outside of the will of His Father's mission.

We must learn that even though we have the ability to operate in the power of God through the Holy Spirit, we should always make sure we are in God's will by being in His perfect timing.

Operating in God's will is very important and a key point in **Ephesians 5:17:**

Therefore do not be foolish, but understand what the Lord's will is.

We are instructed to always understand what the Lord's will is in everything we do. The same way Christ never placed His will for

His ministry over God's purpose, we should not place our will over our Apostle's or Pastor's mission of the local church.

Have there been times in which you wanted to do something in your ministry, and you checked the scriptures and knew what you wanted to do was a God kind of thing to do? Did your idea feel right to you? Did you know in your heart that what you wanted to do would bless others? Did you try to accomplish an assignment without acknowledging or getting permission from your church leader? If you did, you were out of order and not in the will of God. Too many of us have done things in ministry with good intentions as we acted out of the will of God. There is a thin line between being in God's will and working out of our own flesh and effort. We need to constantly make sure we stay in the will of God by checking to see if all that we do lines up with the mission of the church set by our Apostle or Pastor.

Take a moment and write down any events in the past that you did out of the goodness of your heart, but you didn't check with your church leader to make sure it lined up with the mission, vision and values of the church.

_____

_____

_____

Please don't beat yourself up if you are guilty about not acknowledging your church leader. However, going forward, you must operate in the order and the will of God. Write a prayer asking for forgiveness to God. He will forgive you and allow you to move on to building His kingdom through ministry service.

_____

_____

_____

One last point must be made about the importance of setting goals and the impact they have on us operating in dedication, commitment and excellence in our ministries. Taking a final look at **Luke 13:31-33:**

At that time some Pharisees came to Jesus and said to him, "Leave this place and go somewhere else. Herod wants to kill you." He replied, "Go tell that fox, 'I will drive out demons and heal people today and tomorrow, and <u>on the third day I will reach my goal.</u> In any case, I must keep going today and tomorrow and the next day — for surely no prophet can die outside Jerusalem!'

Notice in verse 31 some people came to Christ and warned Him to leave because Herod wanted to kill Him. On the surface, if someone told us to leave a certain place to avoid death, we would thank them and head off to safety. However, notice Christ's response. He replied, **"Go tell that fox, 'I will drive out demons and heal people today and tomorrow, and <u>on the third day I will reach my goal.</u>'** He calls Herod a fox. Why do you think Christ called him a fox? Because Christ knew that the Father had sent Him on a mission to do something. He knew the Father had given Him a particular number of days to deliver and heal a certain number of people. In other words, Christ knew that Herod or no one else could harm Him, because He was in the perfect will of His Father. He knew that what He was doing was not His idea. He knew that He was not trying to do good for God. He knew He was in the divine protection, will and blessing of God.

Christ was really saying to the Pharisees: "Look, I know you really are not concerned about my welfare. You are trying to get me off the path of reaching the objective to deliver and heal people. You are trying to stop people from seeing the power and love of God." Christ was telling the Pharisees that He knew they kept a number of how many people were being healed and delivered and how many people they didn't want to be delivered and healed. Christ responded in a way to let them know that He knew how many people were demon possessed and ill just like they did. However, unlike the Pharisees, He didn't take pride in watching people suffer in order for Him to look good in the eyes of others. He wanted them to have the same freedom and power that He had. As a result, He delivered and healed the specified number of people in the time frame that God allowed Him to operate in. We must never let others get us off the path of achieving our goals and fulfilling the mission that we were sent to complete. Christ didn't and we shouldn't.

We must never let others get us off the path of achieving our goals and fulfilling the mission that we were sent to complete. Christ didn't and we shouldn't.

Now, here is a powerful truth found in **Luke 13:33**, where Christ says,

'In any case, I must keep going today and tomorrow and the next day — for surely no prophet can die outside Jerusalem!'

He confidently tells them that He will not be diverted from the task at hand. He tells them that no one can stop Him from reaching His goal. He tells them that He will surely not die! Did you see that? Christ tells them that no prophet can die outside of Jerusalem! How does He know this? How can He make such a bold statement? He can make this statement with boldness because He knows that He is in the will of God, and He is under the protection of God. He also knows that He is resting with the confidence that comes with the completion of His assignment. What a blessing it is to know that the small minded, evil or treacherous people we may encounter can't stop us from serving and reaching our goal in ministry when we are in the will of God.

We should never let someone who is mean or hurtful stop us from completing our ministry assignment. We should know that God has called us to be successful in ministry. Our success is measured by completing our assigned tasks. Our success can't be measured if we don't complete our tasks because we are run off by people within the church who may hurt our feelings. We can't be successful if we don't have the kind of confidence that Christ had when He took on the Pharisees. This confidence can only come from being in God's will by understanding the overall mission of the church, and setting objectives and goals that line up with the mission. Like Jesus, we must make sure we are on the right path and in the right place doing the right things. We need to make sure that we never operate in ministry outside of the will of God. We will never operate outside of God's will in ministry if we always line up with the church's mission, vision and values that are given to us by our Apostle, Pastor or church leader.

Chapter 6 Review and Exercise

1. It is important to know that ministry is more than just helping people, praying for people and praising God. Ministry is also a business.

2. We must never forget that ministry order must line up with church order. All the things we do in ministry must contribute to achieving the mission, vision and values of our church.

3. Structure and order are key ingredients to conducting a business of excellence in a way that can help the church achieve its mission.

4. We must learn that even though we have the ability to operate in the power of God through the Holy Spirit, we should always make sure we are in God's will by being in His perfect timing.

5. We must never let others get us off the path of achieving our goals and fulfilling the mission that we were sent to complete. Christ didn't and we shouldn't.

Spiritual Exercise

1. Write down the key things you have learned from this
    chapter.

    _____

    _____

    _____

    _____

    _____

2. Write a prayer to the Lord to help you think about how
    you can create (or help create) objectives, goals, action
    plans and contingency plans for your ministry.

    _____

    _____

    _____

    _____

    _____

Chapter 7

Church Order Brings God's Blessings

In those days when the number of disciples was increasing, the Grecian Jews among them complained against the Hebraic Jews because their widows were being overlooked in the daily distribution of food. So the Twelve gathered all the disciples together and said, "It would not be right for us to neglect the ministry of the word of God in order to wait on tables. Brothers, choose seven men from among you who are known to be full of the Spirit and wisdom. We will turn this responsibility over to them and will give our attention to prayer and the ministry of the word."

Acts 6:1-4

If you asked the average church member what are an Apostle's or a Pastor's responsibilities in ministry, you would probably get answers like: Visit the sick, heal and pray for the sick, preach sermons, counsel church members in need, preside over all weddings in the church, attend all board meetings, become civically engaged, be the lead server of food to the homeless, be the point person at the church clothing drive, hug members who are hurt, calm members who are mad, personally address all major issues in the church and speak at community events. Now, take a minute, and look at all of these responsibilities. The reality is that most church members think an Apostle or a Pastor should be in charge of all of these duties.

Most church members might even say that an Apostle or a Pastor involved in some or all of these duties cares about the church and the community, and is a good shepherd. In fact, some church members might say that an Apostle or a Pastor who doesn't do all of these tasks doesn't care about the church, and is a bad shepherd. What do you think? Is it possible for one person to be responsible for all of these tasks? Could one person do all of these tasks well? It is sad, but most church members think that a good Apostle or Pastor is one who is always busy doing a lot in the church.

However, the book of Acts provides a clear example of how God wants the Apostle or Pastor of His church to serve. In Acts 6:1-4 at the birth of the church, there are multiple duties that had to be assigned to each church member in order for God's house to operate in purpose, power and peace. These three must be present in a church for it to become all that God wants it to be.

Our goal in ministry should be to make sure we do all we can to operate in purpose, power and peace.

Objectives of all Ministry Decisions

1. Stay in **Purpose**

2. Stay in **Power**

3. Stay at **Peace**

Our goal in ministry should be to make sure we do all we can to operate in purpose, power and peace.

In Acts, we see that the church was growing. There was a concern that the widows of the Grecian Jews were being overlooked during the daily distribution of food. The specific complaint was that the Hebraic Jews neglected the widows of the Grecian Jews. Now, this oversight was a major problem. If the Apostles didn't come up with a remedy for this problem, there may have been a big church split that could have placed the church movement in jeopardy. To find a solution, the church needed top-level attention from the Apostles. However, notice how the Apostles responded. They immediately established order within the ministry. In **Acts 6:2,** the Apostles said,

"It would not be right for us to neglect the ministry of the word of God in order to wait on tables."

In other words, they would have been out of place and their calling if they focused on duties that would cause them to neglect the ministry of the word of God. Do you see the power here? The Apostles said that they too have a place to serve in ministry — and that place is the ministry of the word of God. Yes! That's right! They were supposed to always be in the face of God — getting instructions on what word to give to the people.

However, the Apostles were challenged to show that they cared by making sure the physically felt life sustaining needs of the people were met. Meeting this need was the first opportunity for the Apostles to prove that they cared for the people. Notice how the Apostles responded. They immediately set the order, and more importantly, set the expectations of what the people should expect from their church leaders. The Apostles told the people sternly that, as Apostles of the church, they must stay where their major power comes from, that is, the ministry of the word of God. How many church members do you think jumped up and down with joy when they heard what the Apostles said? Do you think that a praise and worship session started after the announcement? That probably didn't happened.

Acts 6:1-4 also brings light to some things that cause division in the church: The devil can work through a ministry if we let him. We see that the concern was food. Most people get very edgy during meal time when they're hungry. Most of us don't like missing meals or not being able to eat on time. The devil brought up the issue of food through the people. He knew that if he could get the people upset about not being able to eat, this distraction would cause them to focus on solving the problem of an immediate physically felt need. Again, a key point for us to look at is how the devil brought deception into the church. He wanted the people to focus on physical food. He wanted the leaders to focus on physical food as well. He knew that if he could get the Apostles to not focus on the word but on providing food for the people, he had won the battle. Did you get that? Yes! He wanted the Apostles to feed all of the people until the entire congregation was good and full.

So, what is wrong with that? Do you see the trick? Can you spot the deception of the devil? You should have. If he could get everyone focusing on physical needs, he knew the church would never grow in God. The Apostles knew what he was trying to do, so they didn't waste any words or time setting the church's expectations of the responsibilities of the Apostles. Why? Because the Apostles had to go beyond the physical feeding of the people and spiritually feed them. Do you see it?

105

You should! The Apostles knew that the physical food needed to sustain life is only temporary. However, spiritual food is needed as well for the growth in God. Do you see it now? Do you see why it was necessary for them to focus on the ministry of the word?

In **Acts 6:3-4,** we see how the Apostles handled meeting the physical needs of the people:

"Brothers, choose seven men from among you who are known to be full of the Spirit and wisdom. We will turn this responsibility over to them and will give our attention to prayer and the ministry of the word."

Here they not only set the order, they proved that they cared for the people. The Apostles allowed the people to choose the right number of men with certain qualifications to serve restating the truth that they must get back to prayer and the ministry of the word. How beautiful is that? Isn't that awesome? The Apostles acted swiftly in setting the church's expectations and order in the middle of a crisis. The people needed food, but they also needed prayer and the word of God. Believe it or not, the Apostles knew that they could wait on tables. However, they also knew that only they could pray and minister the word. They made sure that they remained true to what only they could do and appointed others to wait on tables, which God ordained other members of the church to do.

Did the Apostles make the right decision? Did they do the right thing? What would be the evidence to support that what they did was in the order of God? Let's look at **Acts 6:5-7:**

This proposal pleased the whole group. They chose Stephen, a man full of faith and of the Holy Spirit; also Philip, Procorus, Nicanor, Timon, Parmenas, and Nicolas from Antioch, a convert to Judaism. They presented these men to the apostles, who prayed and laid their hands on them. So the word of God spread. The number of disciples in Jerusalem increased rapidly, and a large number of priests became obedient to the faith.

First, the proposal pleased the whole group. These scriptures show that the Apostles made the right decision and were in the order of God. Peace was established. Second, the word of God spread, or growth came to the church. In fact, not only did the word spread, the number of disciples increased rapidly. See! The growth of that local ministry in Acts increased because the house was in order — operating in purpose, power and peace. We need to examine our local ministry to see if we have experienced any growth. If we haven't, it is probably because there is no order and structure from church leadership.

Here is something to think about: We should make sure that the Apostle or Pastor of our church is in the calling where his/her power is greatest. We also should make sure that we are placed correctly for us to be in purpose, power and peace with God Almighty.

> *We should make sure that the Apostle or Pastor of our church is in the calling where his/her power is greatest.*

We can't overlook a key point in **Acts 6:3-4:** The Apostles demonstrated leadership by delegating among their second-level leaders.

"Brothers, choose seven men from among you who are known to be full of the Spirit and wisdom. We will turn this responsibility over to them and will give our attention to prayer and the ministry of the word."

The Apostles delegated the decision of who should serve to their second-level of leaders. The Apostles were so in tune with the ministry of the word and prayer that they didn't have time to choose who would serve the food. The Apostles trusted the second-level of leadership to choose the people who would serve by waiting on tables. This decision shows us that they had already structured the lines of authority and responsibility long before this problem occurred. When the problem occurred, they simply adjusted and instituted their order of the ministry to accommodate these new responsibilities. **A key revelation from the Apostle's decision is that their ministry couldn't grow externally, if it couldn't adjust and adapt internally.**

Ministry Leadership Order

Leadership Level 1: Apostles/Pastors – Prayer and Ministry of the Word (Strategic Planners)
↓

Leadership Level 2: Elders – Administrators/Managers of the Ministry (Tactical Overseers)
↓

Leadership Level 3: Deacons – Servers and Workers, Directly with the People (Tactical Implementers)
↓

Leadership Level 4: Helpers – Apprentices and Trainers for Service and Leadership (Ministry Growth)

The choosing of the seven to serve tables is not a trivial matter. It is serious business. In fact, Acts 6:3 says that these servants must be known to be full of the Spirit! This requirement is why we must never take any assignment in ministry lightly. Where ever we are placed in ministry is serious business. Why do you think that one of the requirements to wait on tables is to be full of the Spirit? It is because food and people are very serious business! If you want to see some arguments (especially in the church), put food in front of people, and watch what happens. Not only must the food service line be organized, the people who are serving must know how to deal with people who can become immature, nasty, mean and unruly at times.

What does it mean to be full of the Spirit? What do you think about when you hear people say that someone is full of the Spirit? Do you immediately think of someone speaking in tongues? If you do, then try to place the value of someone serving food who can speak in tongues to people as they stand in line waiting to be served. Is there a lot of value to the person who is being served? Will speaking in tongues change the person's situation of being hungry? Absolutely not! The answer for why someone must be full of the Spirit lies in the truth of **Galatians 5:22-23:**

But the fruit of the Spirit is love, joy, peace, patience, kindness, goodness, faithfulness, gentleness and self-control. Against such things there is no law.

Do you see it? Being full of the Spirit in order to serve means that a person must represent God and always be able to show love, joy, peace, kindness, goodness, faithfulness, gentleness and self-control especially when the people that person is serving are out of control, mean, nasty and unruly. Leaders who serve others in ministry must be able to rise above the emotional instability of the members. This trait is what separates the church from other people and organizations. We show love, joy, peace, kindness, goodness, faithfulness, gentleness and self-control when others outside of the church cannot.

> *Being full of the Spirit in order to serve means that a person must represent God and always be able to show love, joy, peace, kindness, goodness, faithfulness, gentleness and self-control especially when the people that person is serving are out of control, mean, nasty and unruly.*

> *Leaders who serve others in ministry must be able to rise above the emotional instability of the members.*

It takes a special person to control his/her emotions in the midst of others behaving crazy and mean. A person who is full of the Spirit is even-keeled all of the time. A person who is full of the Spirit can handle an insult and give love back to the person who gave the insult. A person full of the Spirit will not allow people to hurt or insult him/her and quit performing the assignment at hand.

Knowing now why someone must be full of the Spirit to serve and wait on tables, how do you feel about the ministry assignment you are currently serving in?

_____

_____

_____

What are the biggest challenges you face in your current ministry assignment when it comes to being able to display the fruit of the Spirit?

_____

_____

_____

Based on Acts 6:1-7, we should begin to view an Apostle's or a Pastor's love and care for us differently. An Apostle or a Pastor should demonstrate his/her love and care for us by being well trained and organized. Apostles and Pastors should not only meet our physical needs but our spiritual needs as well. Church leaders should never neglect their true calling at the expense of a crisis. They must be strategic visionaries in all aspects of the church. They can't advance the ministry without help. This help comes from servers within the church who accept the calling of God to serve. Never think that something you are doing is trivial or meaningless. All the things we do have equal importance in the body of Christ and are key for the church's growth.

> *An Apostle or a Pastor should demonstrate his/her love and care for us by being well trained and organized.*

> *Church leaders should never neglect their true calling at the expense of a crisis.*

What are your views about the responsibilities of your Pastor now? Have they changed? They should have. We must all learn to become a part of our local church through service and ministering to others. If we do, God will advance our personal lives and the growth of our church as well. As we allow our Apostles and Pastors to focus on prayer and ministry of the word, the sermons we hear will not only sound good, they will change our lives. We must never forget that there is nothing more important in our lives than a fresh word from God. That word can't be overlooked at the expense of our physical needs. Both physical needs and spiritual needs are important, but neither should suffer at the expense of the other. In other words, we need to assist our church leaders through service in ministry and all of our needs will be met and exceeded.

As we allow our Apostles and Pastors to focus on prayer and ministry of the word, the sermons we hear will not only sound good, they will change our lives. We must never forget that there is nothing more important in our lives than a fresh word from God.

Both physical needs and spiritual needs are important, but neither should suffer at the expense of the other.

Chapter 7 Review and Exercise

1. Our goal in ministry should be to make sure we do all we can to operate in purpose, power and peace.

2. We should make sure that the Apostle or Pastor of our church is in the calling where their power is greatest.

3. Being full of the Spirit in order to serve means that a person must represent God and always be able to show love, joy, peace, kindness, goodness, faithfulness, gentleness and self-control especially when the people that person is serving are out of control, mean, nasty and unruly.

4. Leaders who serve others in ministry must be able to rise above the emotional instability of the members.

5. An Apostle or a Pastor should demonstrate their love and care for us by being well trained and organized.

6. Church leaders should never neglect their true calling at the expense of a crisis.

7. As we allow our Apostles and Pastors to focus on prayer and ministry of the word, the sermons we hear will not only sound good, they will change our lives.

We must never forget that there is nothing more important in our lives than a fresh word from God.

8. Both physical needs and spiritual needs are important, but neither should suffer at the expense of the other.

Spiritual Exercise

1. Write down the key things you have learned from this chapter.

   _____

   _____

   _____

   _____

   _____

2. Write a prayer to the Lord to help you always be full of the Spirit as you serve in ministry.

   _____

   _____

   _____

   _____

   _____

Chapter 8

Good and Faithful Service Brings Blessings

"His master replied, 'Well done, good and faithful servant!
You have been faithful with a few things;
I will put you in charge of many things. Come and share your
master's happiness!'"
Matthew 25:21

Matthew gives us a good example of what God expects from us as we serve Him in ministry. God is looking for people to serve Him who are **good** and **faithful**. The Greek meaning for the word good is valuable and beneficial. Looking at the meaning of beneficial shows us that we will be setting ourselves up to receive an advantage. We are beneficial when we add value to the ministry that we have been assigned to within the church. We will know when we add value to a ministry as people begin to depend on us and know that we are the best ones to get an assignment done. Have you ever been responsible for a task and everyone depended on you to make sure it got done? Have you ever walked into a room on your job or at church, and when you showed up, everyone clapped, applauded or gave a sigh of relief?

If so, their reactions proved that you added value to the task that needed to be done. It meant that you were the one they knew could do the best job.

God has placed us in certain parts of ministry where we are the ones ordained to add value to that ministry. No one else will be able to do the job or complete the assignment as well as you can. What a blessing it is to know that God has prepared a place for you in ministry where you are the only person who can add value in that area of service in the church. More interestingly, beneficial means that as we serve God, our dedication, commitment and excellence will prove beneficial to God who in turn will bless us for advancing His agenda of His Kingdom. When we are given a ministry assignment, we should approach it with an attitude that we are going to be good.

Now, let's examine the word faithful. Faithful comes from the Greek word, *pis-tos'*, which means to be trustworthy and reliable. In addition to God wanting us to prove our service to Him as valuable and beneficial to His cause, He wants us to be trustworthy and reliable. To be trustworthy and reliable means that our leaders in the church can depend on us to take charge of an assignment, know that we have their best interest at heart and operate as if we were them. Apostles, Pastors and church leaders are looking for people to take a personal stake in what needs to get done.

Apostles, Pastors and church leaders are looking for people to take a personal stake in what needs to get done.

Read the following story, and see if you can see the value in being faithful in your ministry assignments.

There was a father who owned a very lucrative construction business. He built a successful business that was known worldwide as a high quality and very honest enterprise. He was getting older and wanted to retire. He had only one son and wanted to make sure that his son would always be a person of integrity and build high quality houses just as he had. So one day he told his son that he wanted him to build a house. He gave his son $1.5 million to build a high quality house on a piece of land the father owned for 20 years. He gave his son the check and all the subcontractors the son would need to make sure the house was built with the best materials possible.

The son took the money. Instead of spending it to ensure the highest quality materials were used on each part of the house according to the budget his father gave him, he spent less than half the money and pocketed the rest for himself. He cut corners on the quality of the materials. Then, when he finished the house, he called his father to see the finished work. His father arrived, and they walked through the house together.

The son took him from room to room and took a sense of pride in his completed work. After walking through the house and bragging about the workmanship and quality, the son looked at his father and said,

"Oh by the way, who is this house for?" He added, "I know the person will be happy here because I have put a lot of quality in this house!"

The father asked, "Are you proud of your work?"

The son said, "Yes!"

Then, the father asked, "Could this house last for

100 years?"

"Yes!" the son replied.

The father turned to the son and said, "Good. I wanted you to build this house and put the best quality materials in it. I wanted you to spare no expenses because I wanted to present this house to you as a gift." "This house is yours son," the father said. "I spared no expenses and wanted you to build your house so you would know every inch of this house."

He turned around and looked at his son who was in tears. "What's wrong, son?" He asked.

The son said, "Daddy, I cut back on the quality of the materials. I cut back on the craftsmanship. I was wrong. I thought you would be proud of me for saving money and charging a higher rate."

The father looked at the son and said, "I am very disappointed in you. All these years you have worked by my side and you never saw me cut back on the quality of the materials. I always put the highest quality of materials and workmanship into every house I build."

The son agreed with the father and promised he would never do it again. Then the son turned to the father and said, "What will we do with this house? Who can we sell it to?"

The father turned to the son and said, "You are going to live in this house. This is your home, and you must learn to never forget that you should build every house as if you were building it for yourself."

The son hung his head and said, "You are right Daddy. I will never ever cut corners on a house again."

This story happened 25 years ago. After the father died, the son is still building quality houses to this day. The son doubled his father's construction business, and all over the world people are on a waiting list to have him build a house for them.

After reading this story, what is the lesson that you got out of it as it relates to working in ministry?

_____

_____

_____

How will you approach ministry assignments from now on?

_____

_____

_____

The story showed us how we all must take our ministry assignments and projects seriously. We must remember that we must prove ourselves faithful on the small assignments that are given to us by our leaders. In fact, in order to get promoted to bigger things, God says that we must first be faithful, which means being trustworthy and reliable over the little assignments.

To be reliable means that we do what we said we would do. We show up on time, and we complete our assignments on time. When we work on our assignments in this manner, we prove ourselves ready to be promoted by God.

How do you think God feels toward us when we cut corners on ministry assignments? Does He overlook it? Does He have sympathy on us and hope that one day we will get better? The answer to these questions is no! Let's look at **Matthew 25:24-30:**

"Then the man who had received the one talent came. 'Master,' he said, 'I knew that you are a hard man, harvesting where you have not sown and gathering where you have not scattered seed. So I was afraid and went out and hid your talent in the ground. See, here is what belongs to you.' "His master replied, 'You wicked, lazy servant! So you knew that I harvest where I have not sown and gather where I have not scattered seed? Well then, you should have put my money on deposit with the bankers, so that when I returned I would have received it back with interest. Take the talent from him and give it to the one who has the ten talents. For everyone who has will be given more, and he will have an abundance. Whoever does not have, even what he has will be taken from him. And throw that worthless

servant outside, into the darkness, where there will be weeping and gnashing of teeth.'"

Let's look closer at this scripture. The man who was given the least amount of talents decided that he wouldn't do anything with what was given to him. He literally thought that the money was of such a small amount that it was not worth his effort to try to make it grow into a bigger investment. He was hoping God would bless him anyway. Notice how Christ said the owner responded. He calls the servant wicked and lazy. It is easy to see why the owner calls him lazy. But where does the servant being wicked come from? The Greek meaning of the word wicked means evil. How can the man be evil? He only buried the money and hoped God would still bless him.

A deeper study of the word wicked shows us that it means one who tries to trick, act cunningly and give excuses. What we need to understand here is that this servant made excuses for not increasing his master's initial investment. He was lazy, but when he was questioned as to why there was no increase in the initial investment, he lied. In, **verses 24-25** he said,

'I knew that you are a hard man, harvesting where you have not sown and gathering where you have not scattered seed.

So I was afraid and went out and hid your talent in the ground. See, here is what belongs to you.'

This was not the truth. The servant lied and tried to play on his master's kindness. More importantly, what the servant said made no sense at all. He told the master that he was afraid and put the money in the ground. What does putting the money in the ground have to do with the master's ability to gather where he had not scattered seed? Notice how the servant quickly shifted and said to the master, here is what belongs to you. In all honesty, the servant thought so little of the amount of money given to him that he intentionally didn't put any effort into trying to make the money grow.

How often do we have that same attitude when it comes to small tasks or what we think are menial assignments that we have been given? We don't take the assignment seriously because we think no one is going to notice if we do anything or not, because the task is so small and menial. Then, when we are questioned by leadership, we come up with excuses for the reason the assignment was not completed. This is what the servant did. He made up excuses for his lack of dedication, commitment and excellence. God doesn't like excuses. He wants us to stand up to what we said we would do. If we don't do what we said we would do, we shouldn't lie or make excuses. We should own up to our actions and take responsibility.

Notice how the master responded immediately and told the servant he was wicked and lazy. He stopped him in his lying, cunning and excuses. We should learn from this that God hates these three things. However, notice what the master did in **verses 27-30,**

'Well then, you should have put my money on deposit with the bankers, so that when I returned I would have received it back with interest. Take the talent from him and give it to the one who has the ten talents. For everyone who has will be given more, and he will have an abundance. Whoever does not have, even what he has will be taken from him. And throw that worthless servant outside, into the darkness, where there will be weeping and gnashing of teeth.'

He told the servant what he should have done. Why do you think the master said this? He told him this because he trained the servant and expected him to act differently when he received the money. When we don't use the gifts and abilities that God gives us, we are cutting Him short. We aren't giving Him our best. We are cutting corners, and that is evilness, laziness and wickedness in God's sight.

> *When we don't use the gifts and abilities that God gives us, we are cutting Him short.*

The master took the money from the wicked and lazy servant and gave it to the servant who increased his money the most. He then said that the servant with the ten talents would even have abundance on top of that! Do you see it? The master blessed the servant with the ten talents by giving him the wicked lazy servant's one talent and blessed the wise servant above that. Are you ready to be blessed above what you ever thought you could have? Are you ready to be given more from God? If you are, then you need to begin to work in the ministry of God's church and work at it with all your heart.

In this passage of scripture, we see a master, servants, assignments and blessings. The master is a type of Apostle or Pastor. The servants are types of ministry workers, and then there are the blessings the servants received for their work. The master gave the servant with ten talents even more. He gave this servant more because he won the master's heart. The master was so pleased with the servant that he blessed him above what he produced. This is how your Apostle or Pastor will bless you. When you are given an assignment in ministry and make it productive, fruitful and increase it exponentially, you will move on the Apostle or Pastor to give you his or her heart by blessing you and asking God to increase you above what you could ever imagine. You would have proven yourself to be valuable, trustworthy and fruitful.

An Apostle or a Pastor who finds someone like this prays for that person every day. Your Apostle or Pastor will ask God to bless you and increase you with abundance beyond your imagination because he/she needs you to help the ministry be all the Father has called it to be. Your Apostle or Pastor needs you to help the ministry grow. He/she will depend on you to perform as if you were the leader. Your Apostle or Pastor will give you his/her heart because having the leader's heart is best for you. He/she wants you to live a long, healthy life mentally, emotionally, financially and spiritually.

You must do everything you can do to capture and keep the Apostle's or Pastor's heart. Once you get it, your life will change. Your relationship with God will change. Your power in the Spirit will change. Your personal financial situation will change. You will begin to live an abundant life in God. Serving God by working in ministry is what separates a saved person from a prosperous person. Prosperous people serve faithfully in ministry compared to those who are saved and just go to church.

Prosperous people are dedicated, committed and serve in excellence in the local church.

> *You must do everything you can do to capture and keep the Apostle's or Pastor's heart.*

We must never forget that salvation and the Holy Spirit living in us are a free gift from God received immediately when we confess Christ as our Lord and Savior. After salvation, receiving the Holy Spirit and eternal life, we are promised nothing else from God. To experience a full life and walk in prosperity, we must serve Him and become a part of His body: that is the church. To become a part of His body we must serve faithfully in ministry. It is very simple: When you serve in ministry, God smiles on you and moves on the Apostles, Pastors and church leaders to share their anointing and blessings with you. He will move on them to have a special love for you, and they will pray for the best things of God in your life.

God is looking for servants to be a part of His church. God is looking for people who will assist the Apostle or Pastor and church leaders with ministry assignments. When He finds a servant like this, He blesses that person because He needs him/her to complete the assignments that He has ordained in the church. When an Apostle or Pastor develops a love for someone serving in ministry, they make sure that the Father knows that this is someone who is special. When an Apostle or Pastor finds a faithful ministry helper, it is a powerful combination that will accomplish great things and overcome even greater challenges. It is like the great athletic teamwork of Jordan and Pippen, Magic and Kareem, Bird and Ainge, Rice and Montana.

There are many Biblical teams that were powerful and very successful like Moses and Aaron, Joshua and Caleb, David and Jonathan, Elijah and Elisha, Paul and Silas, and Peter and Cornelius. These men were called by God to work together to accomplish a greater cause for Him. Not only did they work together for the good of God's purpose, they had a unique love for each other. We must never forget that it is impossible to accomplish anything in ministry if there is no love among everyone involved in the task at hand.

We must never forget that it is impossible to accomplish anything in ministry if there is no love among everyone involved in the task at hand.

Finally, the best example of a leader giving his heart to a servant is found between Christ Jesus and Peter. Christ knew that Peter was the one who the Holy Spirit would use to head the new church. Christ had already given Peter the keys to the kingdom, but needed to see if He could give Peter His heart. Notice the exchange in **John 21:15-17,**

When they had finished eating, Jesus said to Simon Peter, "Simon son of John, do you truly love me more than these?" "Yes, Lord," he said, "you know that I love you." Jesus said, "Feed my lambs." Again Jesus said, "Simon son of John, do you truly love me?" He answered, "Yes, Lord, you know that I love you." Jesus said, "Take care of my sheep." The third time he said to him, "Simon son of John, do you love me?" Peter was hurt because Jesus asked him the third time, "Do you love me?" He said, "Lord, you know all things; you know that I love you." Jesus said, "Feed my sheep."

Please take note of how Christ Jesus asked Peter three times if he loved Him. Each time Peter replied that he loved Christ Jesus, He gave him a different assignment. First, He told him to **feed the lambs**. Then, He said **take care of my sheep**. Finally, He told him to **feed His sheep.** Christ wanted to be sure that Peter truly loved Him. He was looking to see if they could become a spiritual team and work together to fulfill the calling of God for the universal church. Next, Christ Jesus educated Peter on the different levels of love required at different stages of the spiritual lives of the people he would encounter as he leads them to maturity. He has to show a different level of love for newborn believers, growing believers and mature believers. The different levels of love must be appropriate, or he could stunt the followers' growth or spiritually starve them and cause them to die. Do you see how important it is to know how to love those who follow you in ministry with the appropriate level of love that will help them mature into all that God ever called them to be?

Notice how Christ Jesus asked Peter if he loved Him at each level? The lesson here is that as leaders, we must be able to love people at all levels of their walk in Christianity and ministry service. Certain people will come to serve with us at various levels, but we must make sure that we give them ministry assignments that complement their growth. Peter becomes discouraged the third time Christ asked him if he loved Him. Peter became discouraged because he became aware that Christ showed him the love that He had for him. Christ showed him how He fed and nourished him from the first days that he and his brother Andrew left their fishing business to become disciples. Christ showed him how He took care of him when they traveled throughout the region and needed food, shelter and protection. Peter realized how Christ took care of all their needs while serving with Him in ministry over the previous three years. Peter felt bad because he saw how Christ fed him spiritual words that grew him up to be able to become bold in God. Peter realized that Christ's love for him through all those stages of his growth came with a lot of challenges and offenses to Christ. However, Christ loved him so much that He forgave him each and every time. Peter realized that as he denied Christ three times, he was now being restored by affirming his level of love three times. Christ simply gave Peter His heart. Christ showed Peter by His example how he must love, be patient and forgive those who will be called to serve with him as they lay down the foundation of the church.

Christ gave Peter His heart by instilling in him that all those who will be called to serve with him will fail, make mistakes and even walk away from ministry. However, they will come back, be restored and serve faithfully if he as a leader will demonstrate love for them at the level of their development and growth in Christ. Christ gave Peter His heart the best way a leader can, through the example of offering forgiveness, being patient and showing love to all who are called to serve in ministry.

<u>Leaders give their heart to others through example by:</u>

1. Forgiving others when they fail
2. Being patient when others stall in growth
3. Loving others when they don't want to be loved

Let's go back to one of the first scriptures you saw in this book, **Ephesians 4:11-13.**

It was he who gave some to be apostles, some to be prophets, some to be evangelists, and some to be pastors and teachers, to prepare God's people for works of service, so that the body of Christ may be built up until we all reach unity in the faith and in the knowledge of the Son of God and become mature, attaining to the whole measure of the fullness of Christ.

From here we can see that Apostles, Pastors and other leaders are called to show the love of Christ through our ability to grow in Him as we serve in the body! Finally, watch how God concludes His purpose for leaders and those who have been called to serve in His body to do a great work for Him. Watch this closely! **Ephesians 4:11-16:**

It was he who gave some to be apostles, some to be prophets, some to be evangelists, and some to be pastors and teachers, to prepare God's people for works of service, so that the body of Christ may be built up <u>until we all reach unity in the faith and in the knowledge of the Son of God and become mature, attaining to the whole measure of the fullness of Christ.</u> Then we will <u>no longer be infants,</u> tossed back and

forth by the waves, and blown here and there by every wind of teaching and by the cunning and craftiness of men in their deceitful scheming. Instead, <u>speaking the truth in love, we will in all things grow up into him</u> who is the Head, that is, Christ. From him <u>the whole body, joined and held together by every supporting ligament, grows and builds itself up in love, as each part does its work.</u>

What a beautiful description of what God wants His church to become. God wants us to work together in love so that we can accomplish everything He ever intended the church to become. The key ingredient needed in order for the power of the Holy Spirit to flow through each person with power is love. That's right! Love is the key and that love must flow from the head down. Love must flow from the Apostle or Pastor to key leaders of the church through ministry servers and finally to the Sunday worshipers who are looking and longing for a display of the love of Christ.

> *God wants us to work together in love so that we can accomplish everything He ever intended the church to become.*

As we walk in this type of love, Christ will pour out His power and blessings in our lives so strong we will not have enough room to store His greatness. So, let your Apostle or

Pastor see your zeal, love and determination at your local church, your spirit of dedication, commitment and excellence and your glad heart. Then, watch him/her pour all their love in you! Watch them give their heart to you. Watch your life change! Watch your health get better! Watch your finances go to new levels of abundance! Watch your marriage or love life take off like a rocket. Watch your blessings come down from heaven! Serve in your church and watch God move in your life. Serving in ministry is one of the best forms of worship we can show God. When we begin to serve God, He begins to bless us. So you should begin to serve in your local church. Capture and keep your Apostle's or Pastor's heart and watch your life change for the best with abundant blessings!

Chapter 8 Review and Exercise

1. Apostles, Pastors and church leaders are looking for people to take a personal stake in what needs to get done.

2. When we don't use the gifts and abilities that God gives us, we are cutting Him short.

3. You must do everything you can do to capture and keep the Apostle's or Pastor's heart.

4. We must never forget that it is impossible to accomplish anything in ministry if there is no love among everyone involved in the task at hand.

5. God wants us to work together in love so that we can accomplish everything He ever intended the church to become.

Spiritual Exercise

1. Write down the key things you have learned from this chapter.

   _____

   _____

   _____

   _____

   _____

2. Write a prayer to the Lord to help you always serve in love as you serve in ministry.

   _____

   _____

   _____

   _____

   _____

Epilogue

One of the surest ways to begin the process of releasing your blessings through ministry service is for you to accept Christ Jesus as your Lord and Savior. If you have never done this, repeat these simple words and it will be a done deal. Repeat the following: Lord Christ Jesus as of this very moment, I accept you as Lord and Savior of my life. I now give my life to you to be fashioned for your purpose and glory. Lord, all of these things I have said, I truly believe in my heart and have confessed with my mouth to you. I know now that I have received everlasting life based on the work that Christ has done and will continue to do in my life. Lord Christ, thank you for bringing me to this point of my life where I surrender my all to you. It is in the Holy Spirit through Christ Jesus, I say Amen.

Humbly Yours in Christ,
Apostle Jamie T. Pleasant

Final Notes and Thoughts

Book Dr. Pleasant for a Speaking Engagement

For speaking engagements, please contact Dr. Jamie T. Pleasant at admin@newzionchristianchurch.org or 678.845.7055

Books By Dr. Jamie T. Pleasant

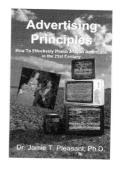

Can be purchased at any bookstore or online at barnesandnoble.com and others

About the Author

Apostle Jamie T. Pleasant; Ph.D. is the Chief Executive Pastor and Founder of New Zion Christian Church in Suwanee, Georgia. He holds a bachelor's degree in Physics from Benedict College in Columbia, South Carolina, marketing studies from Clemson University and an M.B.A. in Marketing from Clark Atlanta University. On August 13, 1999, Apostle Pleasant achieved a Georgia Tech milestone by becoming the first African American to graduate with a Ph.D. in Business Management in the school's 111- year history.

God gave him the vision to establish a Biblically based economic development initiative for New Zion Christian Church. As a result, Apostle Pleasant is constantly sought after and he remains at the pulse of the economic business sector. He created programs in the church such as the Wealth Builders Investment Club (WBIC), which educates and allows members to actively invest in the stock market, along with the much celebrated Institute of Entrepreneurship (IOE), where community members earn a certificate in Entrepreneurship after three months of comprehensive training on aspects of starting and owning a successful competitive business. The main goal and purpose of IOE is that each year one of the trained businesses will be awarded up to $10,000 start up money to ensure financial success. The newly added SAT & PSAT prep courses for children ages 9-19 fuels the potential success of all who walk through the doors of New Zion Christian Church.

Apostle Pleasant has met with political officials such as President Clinton and Nelson Mandela. On April 2010, he delivered the opening prayer for the born again Christian and comedian, Steve Harvey. He has performed marriage ceremonies and counseled numerous celebrated personalities such as Usher Raymond (Confessions Recording Artist), Terri Vaughn (Lavita Jenkins on The Steve Harvey Show), Peerless Price (Atlanta Falcons WR) and many others.

He is civically engaged as well. After the Columbine High School shooting, he founded the National School Safety Advocacy Association. His latest foundations include the Young Entrepreneurship Program (YEP) and the African American Consumer Economic Rights Inc (AACER).

He has authored four books, *Prayers That Open Heaven*, *Capturing and Keeping the Pastor's Heart*, *Powerful Prayers That Open Heaven* and *Advertising Principles: How to Effectively Reach African Americans in the 21st Century*.

Apostle Pleasant is the husband of Kimberly Pleasant and the proud father of three children: Christian, Zion and Nicara.

19150803R00085

Made in the USA
Charleston, SC
09 May 2013